The Life of Ibn Sina

STUDIES IN ISLAMIC PHILOSOPHY AND SCIENCE

Published under the auspices of
the Society for the Study of Islamic Philosophy and Science

THE LIFE OF IBN SINA

A Critical Edition
and Annotated Translation

by

William E. Gohlman

Albany, New York

STATE UNIVERSITY OF NEW YORK PRESS

1974

The Life of Ibn Sina
First Edition
Published by State University of New York Press
99 Washington Avenue, Albany, New York 12210

Printed in the United States of America

Library of Congress Cataloging in Publication Data
Avicenna, 980-1037.
The life of Ibn Sina.
Arabic text and English translation of the author's autobiography, Sīrat al-Shaykh al-Ra'īs, which was completed by al-Jūzajānī.
Originally presented as the editor's thesis, University of Michigan.
Includes bibliographies.
1. Avicenna, 980-1037. I. al-Jūzajānī, ʿAbd al-Wāḥid ibn Muḥammad, 11th cent. II. Gohlman, William E., ed. III. Title.
B751.A5S5 1974 189'.5 73-6793
ISBN 0-87395-226-X
ISBN 0-87395-227-8 (microfiche)

To Susan

ACKNOWLEDGMENTS

MANY PEOPLE have aided me in the research for and preparation of this work, which was originally submitted in partial fulfillment of the requirements for the Doctor of Philosophy in the Horace H. Rackham School of Graduate Studies at The University of Michigan. I would like to acknowledge the following:

The administration of Baldwin-Wallace College, which has provided me with released time from teaching duties and with financial help in the preparation of this work.

Professors Sencer Tonguç and Cengiz Orhonlu of the Faculty of Arts, Istanbul University, as well as the directors of the Suleymaniye and Istanbul University Libraries, who helped me obtain microfilms of the manuscripts I needed. My thanks also to the Ministry of Foreign Affairs and the Ministry of Culture of the Republic of Turkey for giving me permission to do research in the libraries of Istanbul.

And especially Professor George F. Hourani, who provided me with the photographs of one of the manuscripts and gave me a great deal of help and advice in all stages of the preparation of this work.

CONTENTS

INTRODUCTION TO THE EDITION

THE STANDARD ARABIC VERSION of the autobiography of Ibn Sīnā and its continuation by one of his pupils, Abū ᶜUbayd al-Jūzjānī, has been in print since 1884, when August Muller's edition of the *ᶜUyūn al-anbāʾ fī ṭabaqāt al-aṭibbāʾ* of Ibn Abī Uṣaybiᶜa (d. A.H. 668/A.D. 1270) was published.[1] The section on Ibn Sīnā is found in Vol. II, pp. 2–20, and consists of a brief introduction (p. 2), the autobiography of Ibn Sīnā (pp. 2–4), the continuation of the biography by al-Jūzjānī (pp. 4–9), including a short bibliography (p. 5), anecdotes and poems about Ibn Sīnā (pp. 9–10), a number of poems attributed to Ibn Sīnā (pp. 10–18), and a longer bibliography (pp. 18–20).

Another version of Ibn Sīnā's autobiography/biography was published a few years later (1903) in Julius Lippert's edition of the *Taʾrīkh al-ḥukamāʾ* of Ibn al-Qifṭī (d. 646/1248).[2] The material on Ibn Sīnā is found on pp. 413–26, and, like the version in Ibn Abī Uṣaybiᶜa, contains a brief introduction (p. 413), the autobiography (pp. 413–17), and al-Jūzjānī's continuation (pp. 417–26), with the shorter bibliography (p. 418). It does not contain the last three parts of Ibn Abī Uṣaybiᶜa's section on Ibn Sīnā; i.e., the anecdotes and poems about Ibn Sīnā, the poems written by him, and the longer bibliography. In the major sections which the two works have in common, the autobiography/biography, they are almost identical, and so one must suppose that Ibn Abī Uṣaybiᶜa copied this section from al-Qifṭī, or that they both copied from the same unknown source, perhaps a manuscript of al-Jūzjānī's work.

The other major early source for the life of Ibn Sīnā, Ibn Funduq al-Bayhaqī (d. 565/1170), has a section on him in the *Tatimmat ṣiwān al-ḥikma*[3] which contains a great deal of new material and probably not known to either al-Qifṭī or Ibn Abī Uṣaybiᶜa, since neither mentions this material. Ibn Khallikān (d. 681/1282)[4] may have used Ibn Funduq's work, because he includes some material found in Ibn Funduq but not in al-Qifṭī and Ibn Abī Uṣaybiᶜa. However, his biography of Ibn Sīnā is a condensation of the autobiography/biography, with other information interspersed.[5] Ibn al-ᶜImād (d. 1089/1678) follows Ibn Khallikān almost identically in his notice of Ibn Sīnā's life, several times mentioning Ibn Khallikān by name.[6]

Although the accounts in al-Qifṭi and Ibn Abī Uṣaybiᶜa seemed to have been mere copies of the original manuscript which was dictated by Ibn Sīnā to his pupil al-Jūzjānī, and then continued by the latter, several pieces of evidence have turned up recently to show that there is another version of this account. This new text, found in almost identical versions in several different places, does not differ at any major point with the earlier published version, but there are a great number of minor variations. A description of the versions of this new text follows.

In one of the volumes of the *Avicenna Memorial*, A. F. al-Ahwānī mentions the discovery of a new version of the autobiography/biography which differs from the one in al-Qifṭī and Ibn Abī Uṣaybiᶜa.[7] He found this version, written by Yaḥyā ibn Aḥmad al-Kāshī (d. after 754/1353), on the margins of a manuscript of Shahrazūrī's *Nuzhat al-arwāḥ*,[8] which itself contains an account of Ibn Sīnā's life which sounds very much like that of Ibn Khallikān.[9] Al-Ahwānī notes that al-Kāshī's version must merely be a copy of a manuscript similar to the one(s) used by al-Qifṭī and Ibn Abī Uṣaybiᶜa,[10] and so in his edition of it he notes the variant readings of al-Qifṭī and/or Ibn Abī Uṣaybiᶜa. However the edition of al-Ahwānī is not a critical edition of the manuscript itself, since his notes merely carry out his intention of comparing the two versions, and he makes his corrections, emendations, etc., without mentioning them in the notes. This published version of al-Kāshī, called N in the English sections of this work and ن in my Arabic edition (from the title of the published work, *Nukat fī aḥwāl. . . .*), contains the autobiography of Ibn Sīnā (pp. 9–17), the continuation by al-Jūzjānī (pp. 17–28), but without the shorter bibliography, the longer bibliography (pp. 29–35), similar to the one in Ibn Abī Uṣaybiᶜa, and the colophon (p. 36), giving the date as 15 Jumādā II 754 [Thursday, 18 July, 1353].

Another publication of a version different from that of al-Qifṭī and Ibn Abī Uṣaybiᶜa was made by Saᶜīd Nafīsī, who also added a Persian translation.[11] Although Nafīsī states in his introduction the source of his edition: Yildiz Hususi Library (Istanbul), MS. 889, now a part of the Arabic collection of Istanbul University, MS. 4755,[12] he does not provide a critical edition of the work. Rather, he includes a few words in parentheses which represent some of the marginal additions to the manuscript, but there is no indication of any other corrections which he made. I have been able to obtain photographs of this manuscript and so have not had to rely on the published version of Nafīsī. The full description of this manuscript is as follows: Universite, MS. 4755(24), fols. 308a–317b. Written in *nashkhī* script, 16x24 cm. (12x16 cm. each page), 15 lines/page, this manuscript is dated 588/[1192].[13] Called B in the English and ب in the Arabic sections of this work, it contains the autobiography (fols. 308a–311a), the continuation by al-Jūzjānī (fols. 311a–316a), without the shorter bibliography, and the longer bibliography (fols. 316a–317b).

In addition, the most complete bibliography of Ibn Sīnā's writings, Yahya Mahdavi's *Fihrist-i muṣannafāt-i Ibn Sīnā*, lists a number of other manuscripts of the "*sar-gudhasht*" in the libraries of Istanbul.[14] I have been able to obtain microfilms or photographs of several of these manuscripts, the descriptions of which are as follows:

1. Aya Sofya, MS. 4852(1), fols. 1b–13a. Written in large, clear *naskhī* script, 16 × 24 cm. (10 × 16 cm. each page), this manuscript is dated from the first part of the 7th/13th century.[15] Called A in the English and ا in the Arabic sections of this work, it contains the autobiography (fols. 1b–4b), the continuation by al-Jūzjānī (fols. 4b–13a), with the longer bibliography appearing where the shorter bibliography does in al-Qifṭī and Ibn Abī Uṣaybiʿa (fols. 5a–8a), and the shorter bibliography missing.

2. Ahmet III, MS. 3447(6), fols. 20b–26b. Written in clear *taʿlīq* script, 23 × 31 cm., 17 lines/page, this manuscript is dated 866/[1462].[16] Called J in the English and ج in the Arabic sections of this work, it contains the autobiography (fols. 20b–22a), the continuation by al-Jūzjānī (fols. 22a–26b), with the longer bibliography appearing as in A (fols. 22b–23b), and the shorter bibiliography missing. It also includes a number of comments on the margins.

3. Aya Sofya, MS. 4829(19), fols. 72b–75b. Written in large *naskhī* script, 25 × 36 cm., 35 lines/page, this manuscript dates from the 10th/16th century.[17] It contains the autobiography (fols. 72b–73a), the continuation by al-Jūzjānī (fols. 73a–75b), with the longer bibliography appearing as in A (fols. 73b–74a), and the shorter bibliography missing. This manuscript derives from A, containing all of the errors of A and peculiar errors of its own, so I have not used it in my edition.[18]

4. Nuruosmaniye, MS. 4894(44), fols. 247b–250b. Written in *naskhī* script, 23 × 35 cm., 37 lines/page, this manuscript is dated as "possibly" 10th/16th century.[19] It contains the autobiography (fols. 247b–248a), the continuation by al-Jūzjānī (fols. 248a–250b), with the longer bibliography appearing as in J (fols. 248a–249a), and the shorter bibliography missing. This manuscript is derived from J, incorpora-

ting the marginal material found in J into its text, so I have not used it in my edition.

5. Universite, MS. 1458(26), fols. 71b–75a. Written in *taʿlīq* script, 36 × 21 cm., 29 lines/page, this manuscript is dated 1236/[1821].[20] It contains the autobiography (fols. 71b–72b), the continuation by al-Jūzjānī (fols. 72b–75a), with the longer bibliography appearing as in J (fols. 72b–73b), and the shorter bibliography missing. This manuscript, like the one just previously described, is derived from J, including J's marginalia as part of its text, so I have discarded it in this edition.

6. Ali Emiri Efendi, MS. 4353(5), fols. 42b–45a. Written in *taʿlīq* script, 10-1/2 × 15 cm,, 17 lines/page, this manuscript is dated 936/[1530].[21] It contains only the autobiography of Ibn Sīnā and is derived from al-Qifṭī (Q), Ibn Abī Uṣaybiʿa (IAU), or the source(s) which they used, so I have not used it in this edition.

There is another manuscript in Istanbul which Mahdavi calls a "*sar-gudhasht*" of Ibn Sīnā, but it appears to be a condensation of Ibn Funduq's notice of Ibn Sīnā in the *Tatimma*.[22] The author of this abridgement is called Tāj al-Dīn al-Fārisī on the margin of fol. 5a, and in the body of the text on this and other pages he says, "the author of the *Tatimma* said ..." ("*qāla ṣāḥib al-tatimma* ..."). He follows Ibn Funduq closely through the autobiographical section (fols. 1b–3a), then inserts a long bibliography—far longer than the one in this location in Ibn Funduq—(fols. 3a–4a), then skips all of the material in Ibn Funduq down to the description of Ibn Sīnā's last illness and death (fols. 4b–5a). This manuscript, then, was not included in my edition of this work.

Based on the previous descriptions of the surviving manuscripts, the witnesses may be arranged into the following stemma:[23]

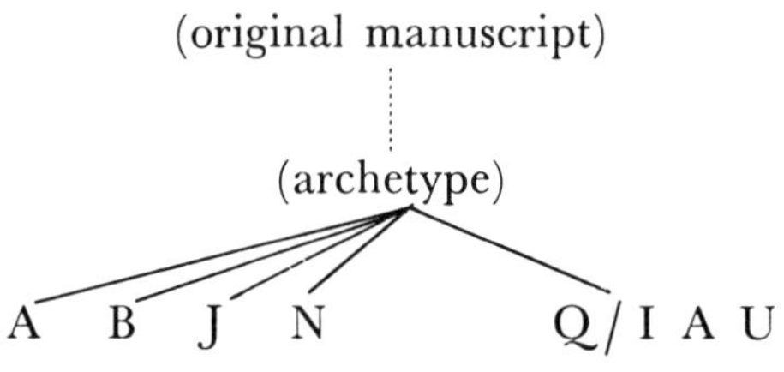

The major split in the manuscript tradition is between Q/IAU on the one hand and A, B, J, and N on the other. I have considered Q and IAU to be a single witness, because there is almost no disagreement between them and they do contain numerous separative errors which are also conjunctive. For example, on page 20, line 7, there is a lacuna in Q/IAU: the word بقراءة is omitted. Since the sentence is grammatically correct without the word, no copyist would likely have added it to the text, therefore A, B, J, and N are not dependent on Q/IAU.

There are also a great many differences of a stylistic nature between the two traditions. At some point Q/IAU was extensively revised and reworked from the point of view of style. The basic meaning of a particular passage remains the same, but word order, verb tenses, and even specific words themselves have been changed by someone who was not just a copyist, but an editor who felt that the passage in question could be improved. I think that this was very likely done by al-Qifṭī, since he was certainly more than a manuscript copyist and would therefore be more concerned with correcting and improving a manuscript than a copyist would. In any case, Q/IAU must be considered quite independent from the other witnesses.

These other sources—A, B, J, and N—must be considered as separate witnesses, since each has at least one separative error against all the rest:

As the oldest manuscript, B could not have derived from any of the other witnesses, nor did any other witness derive from it. There is a separative error against all other witnesses on page 18, line 7, where B has منّى, and all other witnesses have نفسى .

There is a separative error in A against all other witnesses on page 64, line 5, where A has بينهم and all other witnesses have بتنعيم .

There is a separative error in N against all other witnesses on page 74, lines 1–2, where N omits a sentence by homoioteleuton which all of the other witnesses contain, and which could not have been added by a copyist. Since only J is dated later than N, this error shows that J does not depend directly on N, nor does it depend on any of the other witnesses.

A problem arises, however, when we consider the question of contamination of the witnesses. Since Q/IAU and N are printed sources, no subsequent contamination has affected them, and their editors do not specifically mention any previous contamination of the manuscripts from which they prepared their editions. On the other hand, there is evidence of contamination in all three of the manuscript witnesses which I have used in preparing this edition. The most heavily contaminated is B, which contains additions and corrections in the text itself (alteration or crossing out of words—see, e.g., page 42, line 5 in the apparatus), between the lines of the text (lacunae are filled in—see page 42, line 1 in the apparatus), and in the margins (alternate readings are provided—see page 26, line 1 in the apparatus).

There is less contamination in the text of J than there is in B, but J contains a great many marginal notes, some of which provide additional information (see page 16, n. 1, where the name of Ibn Sīnā's mother is given), and some of which make corrections in the text (see page 30, line 1 in the apparatus.) The least contaminated is A, but it does have some words added between the lines to fill lacunae (see page 54, line 9 in the apparatus) and some marginal additions (see page 74, line 7 in the apparatus.)

In preparing the edition, I have treated A, B, J, and N as independent witnesses of one manuscript tradition and Q/IAU (designated as ق/ص in the apparatus) as the witness of the second tradition. Since, as stated above, Q/IAU is more likely to have been revised than the other witnesses, I have followed the latter and listed the variants from Q/IAU in the apparatus. Where the manuscript witnesses have different readings, I have followed the one or more which agree with Q/IAU; where Q and IAU disagree, I have not listed either variant. I have listed the individual variants of the four other sources, including the marginal and interlinear corrections or additions, and have so noted them in the apparatus. I have not footnoted any of the variants, but have listed them by line number for each page. The chosen reading is listed first, followed by the witnesses containing that reading, then a colon (:), followed by the variant and its witness, then (if there is more than one variant), a colon, the variant, its witness, etc. If there is more than one variant passage in a given line, the two, or more, are separated by a double stroke (//).

I have footnoted the material found on the margins of J which provides additional information (perhaps taken from Ibn Funduq) and have placed it below the apparatus in separate notes. Other marginal or interlinear material in J which provides additions or corrections to the text I have placed in the apparatus.

I have not listed minor variants such as differences in the placement and number of dots in a word, ئ (*yāʾ*) rather than ء (*hamza*) in the middle of a word, use of ا rather than ى (or vice versa) as a final *alif*, or other orthographic variants which do not alter the meaning of the text. I have added ّ (*shadda*), initial أ or إ, and have vocalized passive verbs and any doubtful readings.

I have included in my edition the autobiography, the continuation by al-Jūzjānī, with the inclusion of the shorter bibliography (which seems to have been compiled by al-Jūzjānī and is found only in Q/IAU), concluding with the longer bibliography.

The following is a comparison of the order of the contents found in the witnesses, as well as the order of the contents of this edition (1 = the autobiography; 2a & 2b = al-Jūzjānī's biography, sometimes interrupted by 3 or 4; 3 = the shorter bibliography; 4 = the longer bibliography):

Q/IAU	1,	2a,	3,	2b,	poems, and anecdotes,	4	(last two in IAU only)
A	1,	2a,	4,	2b			
B	1,	2a,	2b,	4			
J	1,	2a,	4,	2b			
N	1,	2a,	2b,	4			
This edition	1,	2a,	3,	2b,	4		

In both the edition and translation the introductory material of the various witnesses was omitted, so that the first words of both are those of Ibn Sīnā, beginning his autobiography. For completeness' sake, I give the introductions of the various sources below, first in Arabic, then in translation.

القفطى : **أبو علىّ بن سينا** الشيخ الرئيس وإنّما ذكرته ههنا لأن كنيته أشهر من اسمه سأله رجل من تلاميذه عن خبره فأملى عليه ما سطره عنه وهو أنّه قال: (صفحة ٤١٣)

ابن أبى أصيبعة : (الشيخ الرئيس ابن سينا) هو أبو على الحسين بن عبد الله بن الحسن بن على بن سينا وهو وان كان أشهر من أن يذكر وفضائله أظهر من أن تسطر فانه قد ذكر من أحواله ووصف من سيرته ما يغنى غيره عن وصفه ولذلك اننا نقتصر من ذلك على ما قد ذكره هو عن نفسه وعلى ما قد وصفه أبو

عبيد الجوزجانى صاحب الشيخ ايضا من أحواله وهذا جملة ما ذكرة الشيخ الرئيس عن نفسه نقله عنه أبو عبيد الجوزجانى قال الشيخ الرئيس: (الجزء الثانى. صفحة ٢)

أ: بسم الله الرحمن الرحيم عونك اللهمّ يا قيوم فى سيرته وفهرست كتبه وما وجب تقديمه من مصنفّاته. نكت جمعها الشيخ أبو عبيد عبد الواحد الجوزجانى فى أحوال الشيخ الرئيس حجّة الحقّ أبى على الحسين بن عبد الله بن سينا رضى الله عنه وتواريخه المعروف بسر كذشت. قال أبو عبيد « حدّثنى الشيخ الرئيس أبو على قال: » (صفحة ١ ظ)

ب: سيرة الشيخ الرئيس رحمه الله وفهرست كتبه

وذكر أحواله وتواريخه المعروف بسر كذشت. قال أبو عبيد عبد الواحد الجوزجانى رحمه الله «حدّثنى الشيخ الرئيس أبو على رحمه الله قال: » (صفحة ٣٠٨ و)

ج: مناقب الشيخ الرئيس أبى على بن سينا رحمه الله

بسم الله الرحمن الرحيم قال أبو عبيد « حدّثنى الشيخ الرئيس أبو على قال: » (صفحة ٢٠ ظ)

ن: نكت في احوال الشيخ الرئيس أبى على بن سينا

بسم الله الرحمن الرحيم. نكت جمعها الشيخ أبو عبيد عبد الواحد الجوزجانى فى أحوال الشيخ الرئيس حجّة الحقّ أبى على بن عبدالله بن سينا رضى الله عنه وتواريخه المعروف بسركذشت. قال أبو عبيد: حدّثنى الشيخ الرئيس أبو على قال: (صفحة ٩)

Q: *Abū ʿAlī Ibn Sīnā*, The Shaykh al-Raʾīs (Master and Leader), whom I have mentioned here [rather than earlier in this work, under his *ism*, al-Ḥusayn] because his *kunya* [Abū ʿAlī] is better known than his *ism*. One of his pupils asked him about his past, and so he dictated what has been recorded from him to him [the pupil], which was that he said: (p. 413)

IAU: *The Shaykh al-Raʾīs Ibn Sīnā*, who was Abū ʿAlī al-Ḥusayn ibn ᶜAbd Allāh ibn al-Ḥasan ibn ᶜAlī ibn Sīnā, and who was too famous to need mentioning and whose merits were too obvious to need to be recorded. He related his experiences and described his life so that everyone else can dispense with his own account. And therefore we have confined ourselves for that reason to what he related about himself and also to those of his experiences described by Abū ᶜUbayd al-Jūzjānī, the companion of the Shaykh. This is the sum of what the Shaykh al-Raʾīs related about himself, from whom Abū ᶜUbayd al-Jūzjānī has passed it on. The Shaykh al-Raʾīs said: (Vol. II, p. 2)

A: In the name of God, the Merciful, the Compassionate, [We ask] your aid, O Everlasting God, in [presenting] this biography, the bibliography of his writings, and the compositions of his which must be set forth.

The Shaykh Abū ᶜUbayd ᶜAbd al-Wāḥid al-Jūzjānī has covered well everything concerning the experiences of the Shaykh al-Raʾīs, Proof of the Truth, Abū ᶜAlī al-Ḥusayn ibn ᶜAbd Allāh ibn Sīnā (may God be pleased with him) and his history, known as "*sar-gudhasht*" [a Persian term meaning "recollections"]. Abū ᶜUbayd said, "The Shaykh al-Raʾīs, Abū ᶜAlī said to me": (fol. 1b)

B: *The Biography of the Shaykh al-Raʾīs* (*may God be merciful to him*), *the Bibliography of his Writings*, and the relation of his experiences and history, known as "*sar-gudhasht.*" Abū ᶜUbayd ᶜAbd al-Wāḥid al-Jūzjānī (may God have mercy on him) said, "The Shaykh al-Raʾīs Abū ᶜAlī (may God have mercy on him) said to me": (fol. 308a)

J: *The Attainments of the Shaykh al-Raʾīs Abū ᶜAlī Ibn Sīnā* (*may God be merciful to him*). In the name of God, the Merciful, the Compassionate; Abū ᶜUbayd said, "The Shaykh al-Raʾīs Abū ᶜAlī said to me": (fol. 20b)

N: *Stories Concerning the Experiences of the Shaykh al-Raʾīs Abū ᶜAlī Ibn Sīnā.* In the name of God, the Merciful, the Compassionate; the Shaykh Abū ᶜUbayd ᶜAbd al-Wāḥid al-Jūzjānī has covered well everything concerning the experiences of the Shaykh al-Raʾīs, Proof of the Truth, Abū ᶜAlī ibn ᶜAbd Allāh ibn Sīnā (may God be pleased with him) and his history , known as "*sar-gudhasht.*" Abū ᶜUbayd said, "The Shaykh al-Raʾīs Abū ᶜAlī said to me": (p. 9)

INTRODUCTION TO THE TRANSLATION

IN ADDITION to the earlier Arabic printed versions of the autobiography/biography of Ibn Sīnā, an English translation of this work by the late Arthur J. Arberry has been available since 1951.[24] Professor Arberry's translation was made from the versions of al-Qifṭī and/or Ibn Abī Uṣaybiᶜa—probably from the former, since he follows al-Qifṭī in the only major discrepancy between the two works[25]—so he was unable to take advantage of the new versions published by al-Ahwānī and Nafīsī.

Arberry's translation also contains a number of minor errors, such as "four dirhams" (p. 12) for "three dirhams" (al-Qifṭī, p. 416, line 1), "of a generous format" (p. 22) for "Firᶜawnī quarto" (al-Qifṭī, p. 424, line 12), and various misspellings of proper names, such as "al-Barqī" (p. 13) for "al-Baraqī", "ᶜAnāz" (p. 16) for "ᶜAnnāz", and "al-Karkh" (p. 22) for "al-Karaj."[25]

But the most important reason to undertake another translation of Ibn Sīnā's autobiography/biography is that Arberry, by accident or design, left several lacunae in his translation. Minor omissions occur on pages 14 and 18, where Arberry leaves out verses of poetry, and on page 21, where he omits two anecdotes about Ibn Sīnā's experiences in medical treatment which are included in all of the texts.[27] One other omission is more serious: Arberry does not mention the bibliography which al-Jūzjānī included in the body of his biography of Ibn Sīnā and which both al-Qifṭī and Ibn Abī Uṣaybiᶜa repeat. In addition, the extended bibliography added by a later copyist and included in Ibn Abī Uṣaybiᶜa is not referred to by Arberry in his translation. Neither of these lists, then, has been translated or compared with the modern bibliographies of Ibn Sīnā's works.

Other than Arberry's translation, which has appeared in a number of other places since its original publication,[28] there has been no translation of the autobiography/biography per se. There have been paraphrases, with some direct quotations interspersed, of al-Qifṭī, Ibn Abī Uṣaybiᶜa, or Arberry by several authors. Soheil M. Afnan, in his *Avicenna: His Life and Works*, essentially paraphrases al-Qifṭī and Ibn Abī Uṣaybiᶜa, adding material from Ibn Funduq and Niẓāmī ᶜArūḍī's *Chahār maqāla.*[29] Hossein Nasr, in his *Three Muslim Sages*, has a brief biography of Ibn Sīnā which includes several doubtful conjectures about his life and times.[30] The latest biographical sketch of Ibn Sīnā's life appears in Philip K. Hitti's *Makers of Arab History*, where al-Qifṭī and Ibn Abī Uṣaybiᶜa are given as the sources of his account.[31]

This new translation, then, incorporates those changes in the text necessitated by the discovery of the previously unknown or neglected manuscripts. It also attempts to correct the errors and fill the lacunae found in the Arberry translation, especially by adding the two bibliographies which exist in the medieval sources. The footnotes found in the body of the translation contain material which was found in one or more of the manuscripts, but which did not have enough authority to be included in the text itself.

The "Notes to the Translation" have two major functions: (1) to identify more fully the people and places mentioned only in passing by Ibn Sīnā or al-Jūzjānī. This has been done by using the principal biographical and geographical dictionaries of the medieval Islamic world (as well as modern reference works), and the two most important and complete Muslim historians who dealt with Ibn Sīnā's period, Ibn al-Athīr and Gardīzī; and (2) to amplify what is—very likely deliberately—a skeletal autobiography/biography, one which only hints at or alludes to a great many important events in the life of Ibn Sīnā. This process of amplification was done primarily by quoting or paraphrasing other accounts of Ibn Sīnā's life, or events within that life, using especially the accounts of Ibn Funduq and Niẓāmī ᶜArūḍī. The first of these two men was quite hostile to Ibn Sīnā and the second was too fond of a good didactic anecdote to worry a great deal about its accuracy, but both of their accounts, if used carefully, can shed some light on the obscure parts of Ibn Sīnā's autobiography and biography.

INTRODUCTION TO THE BIBLIOGRAPHIES

Although the bibliographies included in the early sources of Ibn Sīnā's autobiography/biography were edited as part of the complete editions of al-Qifṭī and Ibn Abī Uṣaybiᶜa, less attention has been paid to them since that time. Arberry, as noted above, did not translate the shorter bibliography found in al-Qifṭī and Ibn Abī Uṣaybīᶜa and did not mention either the shorter or longer bibliography in this work. Father Anawati, in his long descriptive bibliography of Ibn Sīnā's works,[32] does not mention either of these early bibliographies, nor do Afnan and Nasr in their studies of Ibn Sīnā's life and works.

Yahya Mahdavi, however, does use these bibliographies to help date some of the works whose dates of composition are not mentioned in the autobiography or the biography by al-Jūzjānī. In fact, he includes an appendix[33] in which he notes which of Ibn Sīnā's works were mentioned in the earliest bibliographies. He includes in this appendix the titles found in al-Qifṭī, the longer bibliography from Ibn Abī Uṣaybiᶜa, two bibliographies from manuscripts found in Istanbul—the two called A and B in this edition—and bibliographies found in two places in Ibn Funduq, comparing all of these with the titles in his own bibliography.

What emerges from a study of these bibliographies is the discovery that the list of works attributed to Ibn Sīnā has grown from "about forty" in al-Jūzjānī's compilation[34] to 276 in Father Anawati's bibliography. However, Father Anawati notes that a number of these are of doubtful attribution to Ibn Sīnā and some of them are clearly by other authors.[35] Mahdavi's list is cut to 132 works which are definitely, by Ibn Sīnā and another 110 which are by other authors, or are extracts from or abridgements of sections of Ibn Sīnā's larger works, especially the *Shifāᵓ*. This posthumous growth of Ibn Sīnā's bibliography began quite early, though, and can be seen in our oldest sources.

The person who added the longer bibliography to the manuscripts must have done so prior to 588/1192, the date of the earliest manuscript, B (although A, too, is dated by Mahdavi toward the end of the 6th/12th or the beginning of the 7th/13th century.) At the time he compiled the longer bibliography, he was able to find ninety-two works, which he then set down and which replaced the shorter list made by al-Jūzjānī in all of the manuscripts (except the one used by Q/IAU.) A parallel process occurred to the manuscripts of Ibn Funduq: a shorter bibliography was supplemented by a longer one. When Ibn Funduq wrote the *Tatimma* (before 565/1169-70), he included in his section on Ibn Sīnā a bibliography containing thirty-eight works, one of which was mentioned twice.[36] However later copies of the manuscript contain a much longer bibliography, which has 118 titles, and which the modern editor of the *Tatimma* has placed in the supplementary notes at the end of the volume.[37]

Ibn Funduq's lists are not identical with those found in Q/IAU and in the manuscripts; his shorter bibliography omits eleven titles found in al-Qifṭī, but adds four other titles not found in al-Qifṭī or Ibn Abī Uṣaybiʿa.[38] His longer bibliography omits twenty-eight of the ninety-two found in most of the manuscripts, but adds fifty titles not included in the longer bibliographies of the manuscripts.[39] This longer bibliography of the later manuscripts of Ibn Funduq is itself supplemented in the brief notice of Ibn Sīnā's life taken largely from the *Tatimma*.[40] This bibliography, written down in 657/1259 (Anawati) or 697/1298 (Mahdavi), contains all of the titles of Ibn Funduq's longer bibliography and adds another thirty titles to these.

This process of adding titles continued in the manuscripts of the autobiography/biography as well; by the time Ibn Abī Uṣaybiʿa wrote down his list, the longer bibliography had grown to 102 items, several of which were probably duplicates under slightly different titles. The manuscript J, which has a large number of marginal notes, contains another eighty titles on the margins of fol. 23b. Since J is dated 866/1462, and another manuscript, Nurosmaniye MS. 4894(44), dated "possibly" in the 10th/16th century, is derived from J and incorporates these added titles into the body of its text, these new titles must have been added to J sometime in the late 9th/15th century or sometime during the 10th/16th century.[41]

If one were to collate all of the bibliographies of Ibn Sīnā's works which were compiled between the 5th/11th and the 10th/16th centuries, the result would be a list of titles approaching 200 in number. How did the number of Ibn Sīnā's works grow so profusely in the first five centuries after his death? The process was very likely the same one which produced a bliography of 276 works in Father Anawati's compilation, but which in Mahdavi's list turned out to be 132 titles. Many of the works of Ibn Sīnā were undoubtedly given different titles by the early bibliographers, and many works listed by them were written by other authors. Since all we possess in many cases is just a title, it is impossible to prove the previous statement completely, but the analogy with the modern case makes it seem quite probable. Another cause for the expansion of the bibliography is found in several of the titles in the shortest bibliography, found in Q/IAU: "Conversations," "Letters to...," and "Commentaries on ...," etc.[42] So in many cases the later bibliographers merely expanded what was already implicit in the earliest compilation by al-Jūzjānī.

In treating the bibliographies in this work I have included the shorter bibliography of Q/IAU (noting the differences between them) in the body of the text of the biography, where it was probably placed by al-Jūzjānī. I have also compared the three shorter bibliographies (Q, IAU, and Ibn Funduq) in Appendix I, giving in addition the number of the work as it appears in the longer bibliography and noting any difference in title in Ibn Funduq or the longer bibliography.

I have edited and translated the longer bibliography from the witnesses A, B, J, N, and IAU, following the procedures given above in the "Introduction to the Edition," except that I have considered all five witnesses to be of equal validity. This bibliography has been placed at the end of the autobiography/biography, where it appears in three of the witnesses, B, N, and IAU. I have also, in Appendix II, placed a table comparing the longer bibliographies of the five witnesses with the longer bibliography of Ibn Funduq and the modern bibliographies of Mahdavi and Father Anawati. I have footnoted differences in the titles of Ibn Funduq's bibliography from those of the manuscripts, but have not noted the differences in the titles of the modern bibliographies, nor have I included the titles found in Ibn Funduq's longer bibliography, the manuscript which supplements this list, or on the margins of J, if these titles are not found in the five witnesses used in this edition.

In Appendix III, I have attempted to put many of Ibn Sīnā's works into the chronological order of their composition, but, for reasons given in that Appendix, I have not been able to do so for a great number of his writings.

سيرة الشيخ الرئيس

كان والدى من أهل بلخ وانتقل منهـا إلى بخارى في أيّام الأمير نوح بن منصور واشتغل بالتصرّف وتولّى العمل في أثناء أيّامه بقرية من ضياع بخارى يقال لها خَرْمَيْثَن وهى من أمّهات القرى بتلك الناحية. وبقربها قرية يقال لهـا أفْشَنَة فتزوّج أبى منها بوالدتى[1] وقطن

---

١) سيرة الشيخ الرئيس ا ب: مناقب الشيخ الرئيس أبو على بن سينا ج: نكت فى أحوال الشيخ الرئيس أبى على بن سينا ن

٢) كان والدى ا ب ج ن: إنّ أبى كان ق/ص

٣) الأمير ساقطة ق/ص

٤) من ضياع بخارى يقال لها خرميثن ا ب ج ن: يقال لها خرميثن من ضياع بخارى ق/ص

٥) بتلك الناحية ساقطة ق/ص / / أفشنة ن ق/ص : انشه ١ : آبشنه ب: افسية ج / / فتزوّج ا ب ج ن: وتزوج ق/ص

---

[1] اسمها ستاره

THE LIFE OF THE SHAYKH AL-RAʾIS

My father was a man of Balkh;[1] he moved from there to Bukhārā[2] in the days of Amīr Nūḥ ibn Manṣūr,[3] during whose reign he worked in the administration, being entrusted with the governing of a village in one of the royal estates[4] of Bukhārā. [The village,] called Kharmaythan,[5] was one of the most important villages | in this territory. Near it is a village called Afshanah,[6] where my father married my mother* and where he took up residence

* whose name was Sitāra

بها وتبنّك. وولِدْتُ أنا فيها[1] ثمّ وُلِدَ أخى[2] ثمّ انتقلنا إلى بخارى. وأُحْضِرَ لى معلّم القرآن ومعلّم الأدب وكمّلت العشر من العمر وقد أتيت على القرآن وعلى كثير من الأدب حتّى يقضى منّى العجب.

وكان أبى ممّن أجاب داعى المصريّين ويُعَدّ من الإسماعيليّة. وقد سمع منهم ذكر النفس والعقل على الوجه الذى يقولونه ويعرفونه هم وكذلك أخى. وكانوا ربّما تذاكروا ذلك بينهم وأنا أسمعهم وأدرك ما يقولونه ولا تقبله نفسى وابتدأوا يدعوننى إليه. يجرون

---

١) وتبنّك ا: وسكن ج ن: ساقطة ب / / أنا فيها ا ب ج ن: منها بها ق/ص

٢) وأحضر لى ا ب ج ن: وأحضرت ق/ص

٣) حتّى يقضى ا ب ج ن: حتّى كان يقضى ق/ص

٦) هم ساقطة ج / / كانوا ساقطة ب / /ذلك ساقطة ق / ص

٧) يقولونه ب ج ن ق/ص: يقولون ا / / نفسى ا ج ن ق/ص: منّى ب / / يدعوننى إليه ا ب ج ن: يدعوننى أيضا إليه ق/ص

---

[1] فى صفر سبعين وثلثمائة والطالع السرطان درجة شرف المشترى والقمر على درجة شرفه والشمس على درجة شرفها والزهرة على درجة شرفها وسهم السعادة فى كط من السرطان وسهم الغيب فى أوّل السرطان مع سهيل والشعرى اليمانيّة.

[2] محمود بعده بخمس سنين.

and lived. I was born there,* as was my brother,+ and then we moved to Bukhārā. A teacher of the Qurʾān and a teacher of literature[10] were provided for me, and when I reached the age of ten I had finished the Qurʾān and many works of literature, so that people were greatly amazed at me.

My father was one of those who responded to the propagandist of the Egyptians and was reckoned among the Ismāʿīliyya.[11] | From them, he, as well as my brother, heard the account of the soul and the intellect in the special manner in which they speak about it and know it. Sometimes they used to discuss this among themselves while I was listening to them and understanding what they were saying, but my soul would not accept it, and so they began appealing to me to do it [to accept the Ismāʿīlī doctrines.] And there was

---

* in Ṣafar, 370 [August–September 980]. The ascendant was Cancer, the degree of exaltation of Jupiter; the moon was in its degree of exaltation; the sun was in its degree of exaltation; Venus was in its degree of exaltation; the Lot of Fortune was in the twenty-ninth degree of Cancer; and the Lot of the Unseen was in the first [degree] of Cancer with Canopus and Sirius.[8]

+ Maḥmūd, five years later.[9]

على ألسنتهم أيضا ذكر الفلسفة والهندسة وحساب الهند.[١] ثـمّ كان يوجّهنى إلى رجل يبيع البقل قيّم بحساب الهند[٢] فكنت أتعلّم منه. ثمّ وصل إلى بخارى أبو عبد الله الناتلىّ وكان يدّعى التفلسف فأنزله أبى دارنا واشتغل بتعليمى. وكنت قبل قدومه أشتغل بالفقه والتردّد فيه إلى إسماعيل الزاهد. وكنت من أفْرَه السائلين وقد ألفت طرق المطالبة ووجوده الاعتراض على المجيب على الوجه الّذى جرت عادة القوم به. ثمّ ابتدأت بقراءة كتاب **إيساغوجي** على الناتلىّ

---

١) أيضا ساقطة ن ق/ص // ثمّ كان ا ب ج ن: وأخذ ق/ص

٢) يبيع ا ب ج ن: كان يبيع ق/ص // قيّم ا ب ج ن: ويقوم ق/ص // فكنت ا ب ج ن: حتّى ق/ص

٣) وصل ا ب ج ن: جاء ق/ص

٤) فانزله ا ب ج ن: وأنزله ق/ص // واشتغل بتعليمى ا ج ن: فاشتغل بتعليمى ب: رجاء تعليمى منه ق/ص // وكنت قبل قدومه ا ب ج ن: وقبل قدومه كنت ق/ص

٥) أفره ج: أخره ا: خيره ب: أحزم ن

٧) بقراءة ساقطة ق/ص

---

[١] وكان أبى يطالع ويتأمّل **رسائل إخوان الصفاء** وأنا أيضا أتأمّله أحيانا.

[٢] والجبر والمقابلة يقال له المحمود المسّاحىّ.

also talk of philosophy, geometry, and Indian calculation.* Then he [my father] sent me to a vegetable seller who used Indian calculation+ and so I studied with him.

At that time Abū ᶜAbd Allāh al-Nātilī,[14] who claimed to know philosophy, arrived in Bukhārā; so my father had him stay in our house and he devoted himself to educating me. Before his arrival I had devoted myself to jurisprudence,[15] | with frequent visits to Ismāᶜīl the Ascetic[16] about it. I was a skillful questioner, having become acquainted with the methods of prosecution and the procedures of rebuttal in the manner which the practitioners of it [jurisprudence] follow. Then I began to read the *Isagoge*[17] under al-Nātilī,

---

* My father used to study and ponder over the *Rasāʾil Ikhwān al-Ṣafāʾ* (*The Treatises of the Sincere Bretheren*) and I also pondered over it from time to time.[12]

\+ and algebra, a man called al-Maḥmūd [sic] al-Massāḥī (the Surveyor, or the Mathematician).[13]

فلمّا ذكر لى حدّ الجنس أنّه المقول عل كثيرين مختلفين بالنوع فى جواب «ما هو ؟» فأخـّذته فى تحقيق هذا الحدّ بما لم يسمع بمثله. وتعجّب منّى كلّ العجب وكان أىّ مسئلة قالها تصوّرتها خيرا منه وحذّر والدى من شغلى بغير العلم. حتّى قرأت ظواهر المنطق عليه وأمّا دقائقه فلم يكن عنده منها خبر. ثمّ أخذت أقرأ الكتب على نفسى وأطالع الشروح حتّى أحكمت علم المنطق. فأمّا كتاب أوقليدس فإنّى قرأت عليه من أوّله خمسة أشكال أو ستّة ثمّ تولّيت حلّ بنفسي بقية الكتاب بأجمعه. ثمّ انتقلت

---

١) فلمّا ا ب ج ن: ولمّا ق/ص / / لى ساقطة ن / / أنّه ا ب ج: من أنّه ن: أنّه هو ق/ص

٢) فأخـّذته ا ب ج ن: فأخذت ق/ص / / الحدّ ساقطة ن

٣) قالها ج ن ق/ص : ساقطة ا: ذكرها ب

٣—٤) وكان . . . العلم ا ب ج ن: وحذّر والدى من شغلى بغير العلم وكان أىّ مسئلة قالها لى أتصوّرها خيرا منه ق/ص

٥) وأمّا ا ج ن ق/ص: فامّا ب / / منها ا ب ج ق/ص: منه ن

٧) فأمّا ا ب ج ن: وكذلك ق/ص / / فإنّى قرأت عليه من أوّله ا ب ج ن: فقرأت من أوّله ق/ص

٨) ستّة ا ب ج ن: ستّة عليه ق/ص / / بأجمعه ا ب ج ن: بأسره ق/ص

and when he mentioned to me the definition of genus,[18] as being that which is predicated[19] of a number of things of different species in answer to the question "What is it?", I evoked his admiration by verifying this definition in a manner unlike any he had heard of. He was extremely amazed at me; whatever problem he posed I conceptualized better than he, so he advised my father against my taking up any occupation other than learning. |

I continued until I had read the simple parts of logic under him; but as for its deeper intricacies, he had no knowledge of them. So I began to read the texts and study the commentaries by myself until I had mastered logic. As for Euclid,[20] I read the first five or six figures under him; then I undertook the solution of the rest of the book in its entirety by myself. Then I moved on

إلى **المجسطي** ولمّا فرغت من مقدّماته وانتهيت إلى الأشكال الهندسيّة قال لي الناتليّ « تولّ قراءتها وحلّها بنفسك ثمّ اعرضها عليّ لأبيّن لك صوابه من خطئه. » وما كان الرجل يقوم بالكتاب فحللته. فكم من شكل ما عرفه إلّا حين عرضته عليه وفهّمته إيّاه. ثمّ فارقني الناتليّ متوجّها إلى كركانج.[1]

واشتغلت أنا بتحصيل الكتب من الفصوص والشروح من الطبيعيّات والإلهيّات وصار أبواب العلم تنفتح عليّ. ثمّ رغبت في علم الطبّ وقرأت الكتب المصنّفة فيه. وعلم الطبّ ليس هو من العلوم الصعبة

---

١) وانتهيت ب ج ن ق/ص: وانتقلت ا

٣) خطئه ا ب ن ق/ص: خطأ ج / / فحللته ا ب ج ن: وأخذت أحلّ ذلك الكتاب ق/ص

٤) إلّا حين ا ب ج ن: إلّا (إلى ص) وقتما ق/ص / / وفهّمته ب ج ن ق/ص: وفهّمت ا

٥) كركانج ا ب ن ق/ص: كركالنج ج

٦–٧) الطبيعيّات والإلهيّات ا ب ج ن: الطبيعيّ والإلهيّ ق/ص

٨) وقرأت ا ب ج ن: وصرت أقرأ ق/ص / / فيه ساقطة ا / / هو ساقطة ن ق/ص

---

[1] تلقاء خوارزم قاصدا حضرة خوارزمشاه مأمون بن محمّد

to the *Almagest*,[21] and when I had finished its introductory sections and got to the geometrical figures, al-Nātilī said to me, "Take over reading and solving them by yourself, then show them to me, so that I can explain to you what is right with it and what is wrong." But the man did not attempt to deal with the text, so I deciphered it myself. And many a figure he did not grasp until I put it before him and made him understand it. Then al-Nātilī left me, | going on to Gurgānj.*

I devoted myself to studying the texts—the original and commentaries—in the natural sciences and metaphysics,[23] and the gates of knowledge began opening for me. Next I sought to know medicine, and so I read the books written on it. Medicine is not one of the difficult sciences,

* opposite Khwārazm, seeking the court of the Khwārazm-shāh Maʾmūn ibn Muḥammad.[22]

فلذلك برزت فيه أقلّ مدّة حتّى بدأ فضلاء الأطبّاء يقرءون علىّ علم الطبّ. وتعهّدت المرضى فانفتح علىّ من أبواب المعالجات المقتبسة من التجربة ما لا يوصف. وأنا مع ذلك مشغول بالفقه وأناظر فيه وأنا يومئذ من أبناء ستّ عشرة سنة.

ثمّ توفّرت على العلم والقراءة سنة ونصفا فاعدت قراءة المنطق وجميع أجزاء الفلسفة. ولم أنم فى هذه المدّة ليلة واحدة بطولها ولا اشتغلت بالنهار بغيره. وجمعت بين يدىّ ظهورا فكلّ حجّة

---

١) فلذلك ا ب ج ن: فلا جرم أنّى ق/ص وعلى هامش ب // الأطبّاء ا ب ج ن: الطلبّ ق/ص

٢) أبواب ا ج ن ق/ص: باب ب // المقتبسة ا ب ج ق/ص: المصنّفة ن

٣) مشغول بالفقه ا ب ج ن: أختلف إلى الفقه ق/ص

٤) يومئذ ا ب ج ن: فى هذا الوقت ق/ص // ستّ عشرة ب ن ق/ص: ستّة عشر ا ج

٥) نصفا ب ن ق/ص: نصف ا: نصف سنة ج

٦) ولم أنم فى هذا المدّة ا ب ج ن: وفى هذا المدّة ما نمت ق/ص

٧) فكلّ ا ب ن ق/ص: وكلّ ج

and therefore I excelled in it in a very short time, to the point that distinguished physicians began to read the science of medicine under me. I cared for the sick and there opened to me some of the doors of medical treatment that are indescribable and can be learned only from practice. In addition I devoted myself to jurisprudence and used to engage in legal disputations, at that time being sixteen years old. |

Then, for the next year and a half, I dedicated myself to learning and reading; I returned to reading logic and all the parts of philosophy. During this time I did not sleep completely through a single night nor devote myself to anything else by day. I compiled a set of files[24] for myself, and for each proof

كنت أنظر فيها أثبتّ (فيها) ما فيها من مقدّمات قياسيّة وترتيبها وما عساها تنتج. وأراعى شروط مقدّماتها حتّى تتحقّق لى تلك المسألة. والّذى كنت أتحيّر فيه من المسائل ولا أظفر فيه بالحدّ الأوسط فى القياس أتردّد بسبب ذلك إلى الجامع وأصلىّ وأبتهل إلى مبدع الكلّ
حتّى يفتح لى المنغلق منه ويسهّل المتعسّر. وأرجع بالليل إلى دارى /٥
وأحضر السراج بين يدىّ وأشتغل بالقراءة والكتابة. فمهما غلبنى النوم

---

١) أنظر فيها ا ب ج ق/ص: فيما ن

١–٢) أثبت ... تنتج [كلّ النصوص غالطة]: أثبتّه من مقدّمـــات قياسيّة وترتيبها وما عساها تنتج ا: أثبتّ ما فيها من المقدّمات القياسيّة وترتيبها وما عساها تنتج ب: أثبتّه من مقدّمات قياسيّة ورتّبتها (فى تلك الظهور ثمّ نظرت) فيما عساها تنتج ج (وهامش ج): أثبتته من مقدّمات قياسيّة وترتيبها وما عساها تنتج ن: أثبتّ مقدّمات قياسه (قياسيّة ص) فى تلك الظهور ورتّبتها ثمّ نظرت فيما عساها تنتج ق/ص

٢) وأراعى ا ب ن: وأراع ج: وراعيت ق/ص // مقدّماتها ا ب ج ن: مقدّماته ق/ص // تتحقّق ا ج ن: تنحلّ ب: تحقّق ق/ص

٣–٥) والّذى . . . المتعسّر ا ب ج ن: وكلّما كنت أتحيّر فى مسألة ولم أكن أظفر بالحدّ الأوسط فى قياس ترددت إلى الجامع وصلّيت وابتهلت إلى مبدع الكلّ حتّى فتح لى المنغلق ويسّر (تيسّر ص) المتعسّر ق/ص

٣) ولا أظفر ا ب ج: ولم أظفر ن // فيه ساقة ج ن

٥) يفتح ا ب ج: يتّضح ن // المنغلق ا ج ن: المغلق ب // وأرجع ا ب ج ن: وكنت أرجع ق/ص // بالليل إلى دارى ا ج ن ق/ص: إلى دارى بالليل ب

٦) وأحضر ا ب ج ن: وأضع ق/ص

that I examined, I entered into the files its syllogistic premises, their classification,[25] and what might follow from them. I pondered over the conditions of its premises, until this problem was verified for me. And because of those problems which used to baffle me, not being able to solve the middle term of the syllogism, I used to visit the mosque frequently and worship, praying humbly to the All-Creating | until He opened the mystery of it to me and made the difficult seem easy. At night I would return home, set out a lamp before me, and devote myself to reading and writing. Whenever sleep overcame me

أو شعرت بضعف عدلت إلى شرب قدح من الشراب لكيما تعود إلىّ قوّتى . ثمّ أرجع إلى القراءة . ومهما أخذنى نوم كنت أرى تلك المسائل بأعيانها فى منامى واتّضح لى كثير من المسائل فى النوم. ولم أزل كذالك حتّى استحكم معى جميع العلوم ووقفت عليها بحسب الإمكان الإنسانىّ. وكلّ ما علمته فى ذلك الوقت فهو كما علمته الآن. لم أزدد إلى اليوم فيه شيئا.

حتّى أحكمت العلم المنطقىّ والطبيعىّ والرياضىّ وانتهيت إلى العلم

---

١) الشراب ا ج ن ق/ص: شراب ب / / لكيما ا ب ج ن: ريثما ق/ص وعلى هامشى ب ج

٢) قوّتى ا ج ن ق/ص: قواى ب / / أخذنى ا ب ج ن: + أدنى على هامش ج

٢–٣) ومهما . . . فى النوم. ا ب ج ن: ومهما (متى ق) أخذنى أدنى نوم أحلم بتلك المسائل (المسألة ق) بأعيانها (بعينها ق) حتّى إنّ كثيراً من المسائل اتّضح لى وجوهها فى المنام ق/ص

٣) منامى ا ب ج: نومى ن

٥) الآن ساقطة ا ج ن

٦) إلى اليوم فيه شيئا ا ج ن: فيه شيئا إلى اليوم ب: فيه إلى اليوم ق/ص

٧) العلم المنطقىّ ا ب ج ن: علم المنطق ق/ص / / والرياضىّ ا ج ن ق/ص: ثمّ الرياضىّ ب

or I became conscious of weakening, I would turn aside to drink a cup of wine, so that my strength would return to me.[26] Then I would return to reading. And whenever sleep seized me I would see those very problems in my dream; and many questions became clear to me in my sleep. I continued in this until all of the sciences were deeply rooted within me and I understood them as far as is | humanly possible. Everything which I knew at that time is just as I know it now; I have not added anything to it to this day.

Thus I mastered the logical, natural, and mathematical sciences,[27] and I had now reached the science

الإلهيّ. وقرأت كتاب **ما بعد الطبيعة** فلم أفهم ما فيه والتبس عليّ غرض واضعه حتّى أعدت قراءته أربعين مرّة وصار لى محفوظا . وأنا مع ذلك لا أفهمه ولا المقصود به وأيست من نفسى وقلت « هذا كتاب لا سبيل إلى فهمه. » فحضرت يوما وقت العصر في الورّاقين فتقدّم دلال بيده مجلّد ينادى عليه . فعرضه عليّ فرددته ردّ متبرّم معتقد أنّ لا فائدة في هذا العلم . فقال لى « اشتره فصاحبه محتاج إلى ثمنه وهو رخيص . وأبيعكه بثلاثة دراهم . » فاشتريته فإذا هو كتاب

---

١) فلم أفهم ا ب ج ن: فما كنت أفهم ق/ص

٣) مع ذلك ساقطة ج ن وهى على هامش ج / / به فوق خطّ ج / / من نفسى] + منه على هامش ج

٤) فحضرت يوما ا ب ج ن: وإذا أنا فى يوم من الأيّام حضرت ق/ص

٥) فتقدّم دلال بيده ا ب ج ن: وبيد دلال ق/ص / / مجلّد ا ب ج ق/ص : كتاب ن

٦) أنّ لا ا ب ج ق/ص: ألا ن / / لى ساقطة ب / / اشتره ب ج ن: اشتريه ا

٦–٧) اشتره . . . دراهم ا ب ج ن: اشتر منّى هذا فانّه رخيص أبيعكه بثلاثة دراهم وصاحبه محتاج إلى ثمنه ق/ص

٧) وأبيعكه ا ج ن: أبيعكه ب

of metaphysics. I read the *Metaphysics* [of Aristotle],[28] but I could not comprehend its contents, and its author's object remained obscure to me, even when I had gone back and read it forty times and had got to the point where I had memorized it. In spite of this I could not understand it nor its object, and I despaired of myself and said, "This is a book which there is no way of understanding." But one day in the afternoon when I was at the booksellers' quarter | a salesman[29] approached with a book in his hand which he was calling out for sale. He offered it to me, but I refused it with disgust, believing that there was no merit in this science. But he said to me, "Buy it, because its owner needs the money and so it is cheap. I will sell it to you for three *dirhams*." So I bought it and, lo and behold, it was

أبى نصر الفارابىّ في أغراض كتاب **ما بعد الطبيعة** . ورجعت إلى دارى وأسرعت قراءته فانفتح علىّ فى الوقت أغراض ذلك الكتاب لأنّه كان قد صار لى محفوظا على ظهر القلب. وفرحت بذلك وتصدّقت فى اليوم الثانى بشىء كثير على الفقراء شكرا لله تعالى .

واتّفق لسلطان الوقت ببخارى وهو نوح بن منصور مرض تحيّر الأطبّاء فيه. وقد كان اشتهر اسمى بينهم بالتوفّر على العلم والقراءة فأجروا ذكرى بين يديه وسألوه إحضارى . فحضرت وشاركتهم فى مداواته وتوسّمت بخدمته. وسألته يوما الإذن لى فى الدخول إلى دار

---

١) أبى اب ج ن: لأبى ق/ص / / ورجعت ا ج ن: فرجعت ب
٢) دارى ا ب ج ن: بيتى ق/ص / / لأنّه ا ب ج ن: بسبب أنّه ق/ص
٣) كان ساقطة ن / / وفرحت ا ب ج ق/ص: ففرحت ب
٤) بشىء كثير ب ج ن ق/ص: شيئا كثيرا ا
٥) واتّفق . . . مرض ا ب ج ن: وكان سلطان بخارى فى ذلك الوقت نوح بن منصور واتّفق له مرض ق/ص
٦) الأطبّاء فيه ا ج ن ق/ص: فيه الأطبّاء ب / / وقد كان اشتهر اسمى ا ب ج ن: وكان اسمى اشتهر ق/ص / / العلم و ساقطة ق/ص
٨) مداواته] + صلح على هامش ج / / وسألته ا ب جن: فسألته ق/ص / / فى الدخول إلى دار ا ب ج ن: فى دخول دار ق/ص

Abū Naṣr al-Fārābī's book on the objects of the *Metaphysics*.[30] I returned home and was quick to read it, and in no time the objects of that book became clear to me because I had got to the point of having memorized it by heart. I rejoiced at this and the next day gave much in alms to the poor in gratitude to God, who is exalted. |

It happened that the Sulṭān[31] of that time in Bukhārā, Nūḥ ibn Manṣūr, had an illness which baffled the doctors. Since my name had become well known among them as a result of my zeal for learning and reading, they brought me to his attention and asked him to summon me. Thus I presented myself and joined with them in treating him, and so became enrolled in his service.[32] One day I asked him to permit me to go into

كتبهم ومطالعتها وقراءة ما فيها. فأذن لى وأُدْخِلْتُ إلى دار ذات بيوت كثيرة فى كل بيت صناديق كتب منضّدة بعضَها على بعض. ففى بيت منها كتب العربيّة والشعر وفى آخر الفقه وكذلك فى كلّ بيت علم مفرد. فطالعت فهرست كتب الأوائل وطلبت ما احتجت إليه. ورأيت من الكتب ما لم يقع اسمه إلى كثير من الناس ولم أكن رأيته قبل ذلك ولا رأيته أيضا من بعد. فقرأت تلك الكتب وظفرت بفوائدها وعرفت مرتبة كلّ رجل فى علمه.

فلمّا بلغت ثمانى عشرة سنة من عمرى فرغت من هذه العلوم كلّها.

---

١) ما فيها] + من كتب الطبّ ق/ص // وأدخلت إلى دار ا ب: ودخلت إلى دار ج ن: فدخلت دارا ق/ص

٢) ففى ا ب ج ن: فى ق/ص

٣) منها ساقطة ق/ص

٤) علم مفرد ا ب ج ن: كتب علم مفرد ق/ص: كتب فوق خطّ ب

٥) من الناس] + قطّ ق/ص

٦) رأيته ب ن ق/ص: رأيت ا ج // وظفرت ب ج ن ق/ص: فظفرت ا

٨) ثمانى عشرة ب: ثمانية عشر ا ج: ثمانية عشرة ن

their library, to get to know it and to read its books. He gave me permission and I was admitted to a building which had many rooms; in each room there were chests of books piled one on top of the other. In one of the rooms were books on the Arabic language and poetry, in another, on jurisprudence, and likewise in each room [were books on] a single science. So I looked through the catalogue of books by the ancients[33] and asked for whichever one I needed. | I saw books whose names had not reached very many people and which I had not seen before that time, nor have I seen since. I read these books and mastered what was useful in them and discovered the status of each man in his science.[34]

So when I had reached the age of eighteen I was finished with all of these sciences;

وكنت إذ ذاك للعلم أحفظ ولكنّه اليوم معى أنضج وإلّا فالعلم واحد لم يتجدّد لى شىء من بعد.

وكان فى جوارى رجل يقال له أبو الحسن العروضىّ فسألنى أن أصنّف له كتابا جامعا فى هذا العلم . فصنّفت له **المجموع** وسميّته باسمه وأتيت فيه على سائر العلوم سوى العلم الرياضىّ. ولى إذ ذاك إحدى وعشرون سنة. وكان فى جوارى أيضا رجل يقال له أبو بكر البرقىّ خوارزمىّ المولد فقيه النفس متوجّه فى الفقه والتفسير والزهد مائل إلى هذه العلوم. فسألنى شرح الكتب فصنّفت له كتاب **الحاصل والمحصول** فى قريب من عشرين مجلّدة . وصنّفت له فى

---

١) وكنت إذ ذاك ا ج ن ق/ص: وإذ ذاك كنت ب / / اليوم معى ا ج ن ق/ص: معى اليوم ب / / أنضج ا ب ن ق/ص: أوضح ج

٢) شىء من بعد ا ب: + ذلك ج: من ساقطة ن: بعده شىء ق/ص

٣) أبو الحسن ا ب ج: أبو الحسين ن

٥) باسمه ا ب ج ن: به ق/ص: + الحكمة العروضيّة على ها ش ب / / العلم ساقطة ق/ص

٦) عشرون ب ن ق/ص: عشرين ا ج / /سنة] + من عمرى ق/ص / / أيضا ساقطة ا

٧) متوجّه ا ج ن: متوجّها ب: متوحّد ق/ص

٨) مائل ا ج ن ق/ص: مائلا ب / / الكتب] + له ق/ص

٩) مجلّدة ب ج ن ق/ص: مجلّدا ا

at that time I had a better memory for learning, but today my knowledge is more mature; otherwise it is the same; nothing new has come to me since.

In my neighborhood there was a man named Abū al-Ḥasan the Prosodist,[35] who asked me to compose for him a comprehensive work on this learning [which I had attained.] So I wrote *The Compilation* for him, and gave | his name to it, including in it all of the sciences except mathematical science. At that time I was twenty-one years old. Also in my neighborhood there was a man named Abū Bakr al-Baraqī,[36] a Khwārazmian by birth, and a lawyer by inclination; he was distinguished in jurisprudence, Qurʾān commentary, and asceticism, having a liking for these sciences. He asked me to comment on the books [in these sciences], and so I wrote *The Sum and Substance* for him in about twenty volumes.[37] I also wrote for him a book on

الأخلاق كتابا سميّته كتاخ **البرّ الاثم**. وهذان الكتابان لا يوجدان إلّا عنده فإنّه لم يُعِر أحدا يُنْسَخ منهما.

ثمّ مات والدى وتصرّفت بى الأحوال وتقلّدت شيئا من أعمال السلطان. ودعتنى الضرورة إلى الإخلال ببخارى والانتقال إلى كركانج وكان أبو الحسين السهيلىّ المحبّ لهذه العلوم بها وزيرا.

وقُدّمْتُ إلى الأمير بها وهو علىّ بن مأمون وكنت إذ ذاك علىّ زىّ الفقهاء بطيلسان تحت الحنك. فرتّبوا لى مشاهرة تقوم بكفاية مثلى. ثمّ دعت الضرورة إلى الانتقال إلى نسا ومنها إلى باورد

---

١) كتاب ساقطة ب ولكنّها فوق خطّه

٢) فانّه لم ا ب ج ن: فلم ق/ص // يعر ا ج ن: يعرهما ب // أحدا ب ج ن ق/ص: أحد ا // ينسخ ا ب ج: ينتسخ ن ق/ص // منهما ب ق/ص: منه ا ج ن

٣) بى ب ن ق/ص: فى ا ج

٤) الإخلال ببخارى ا ب ن: الانجلاء من بخارى ج

٥) الحسين ا ج ن ق/ص: الحسن ب // السهيلىّ] — السهلىّ فى كلّ النصوص

٦) إلى ج ق/ص: على ا ب ن // هو ساقطة ب ولكنّها فوق خطّه

٦–٧) إذ ذاك علىّ زىّ الفقهاء ا ب ج ن: علىّ زىّ الفقهاء إذ ذاك ق/ص

٧) تحت ا ب ج: وتحت ن ق/ص // فرتّبوا ا ب ج ن: وأثبتوا ق/ص // مشاهرة] + دارّة ق/ص وعلى هامش ج

ethics which I called *Good Works and Evil.*[38] These two works exist only in his possession, and he has not loaned out either one of them to be copied.

Then my father died[39] and I was free to govern my own affairs and so I took over one of the administrative posts of the Sulṭān. Necessity then led me to forsake Bukhārā and move to Gurgānj,[40] | where Abū al-Ḥusayn al-Suhaylī,[41] an amateur of the sciences, was a minister. I was presented to the Amīr there, ʿAlī ibn Maʾmūn;[42] at that time I was in lawyer's dress, with a fold of the mantle under my chin. They gave me a monthly salary which provided enough for someone like me. Then necessity led me[43] to move to Nasā,[44] and from there to Bāward,[45]

ومنها إلى طوس ومنها إلى سمنقان ومنها إلى جاجرم رأس حدّ خراسان ومنها إلى جرجان. وكان قصدى الأمير قابوس[1] فاتّفق في أثناء ذلك أخذ قابوس وحبسه في بعض القلاع وموته هناك.

ثمّ مضيت إلى دهستان ومرضت بها مرضا صعبا وعدت منها إلى جرجان واتّصل أبو عبيد الجوزجانىّ بى وأنشدنى فى حالى قصيدة فيها البيت للقائل:

لمّا عظمت فليس مصر واسعى لمّا غلا ثمنى عدمت المشترى

١) ومنها إلى سمنقان ا ج: ومنها إلى شقّان ب: ساقطة ن: ومنها إلى شقّان ومنها إلى سمنقان ق/ص / / حدّ ساقطة ا ب ولكنّها فوق خطّ ب
٣) ذلك ا ب ج ن: هذا ق/ص
٤) منها ساقطة ق/ص
٥) وأتصل ا ج ن: فاتّصل بي ب / / بي ساقطة ا ج / / وأنشدني ا: وأنشدني ت ب: وأنشدت ج ن: وأنشأت ق/ص
٦) البيت للقائل ا: البيت القائل ب ج ن: بيت القائل ق/ص

[1] بن وشمكير وهو صاحب جرجان

and then to Ṭūs,[46] then to Samanqān,[47] then to Jājarm,[48] at the extreme limit of Khurāsān, and then to Jurjān.[49] My destination was the Amīr Qābūs,*[50] but at that time there occurred the seizure of Qābūs,[51] his imprisonment in one of his castles, and his death there.

Then I departed for Dihistān,[52] where I became very ill, and from where I returned | to Jurjān. Abū ʿUbayd al-Jūzjānī[53] joined me there and recited to me an ode on my state of affairs which contains the poet's verse:

When I became great, no country could hold me;
When my price went up, I lacked a buyer.

* ibn Wushmagīr, who was the ruler of Jurjān.[50]

قال الشيخ أبو عبيد: فهذا ما حكاه لى الشيخ من لفظة ومن ههنا ما شاهدته أنا من أحواله والله الموفّق.

كان بجرجان رجل يقال له أبو محمّد الشيرازىّ يحبّ هذه العلوم وقد اشترى للشيخ دارا فى جواره وأنزله فيها. وكنت أنا أختلف إليه كلّ يوم فأقرأ **المجسطى** وأستملى المنطق فأملى علىّ **المختصر الأوسط في المنطق** وصنّف لأبى محمّد الشيرازىّ كتاب **المبدأ والمعاد** وكتاب **الأرصاد الكلّيّة** وصنّف هناك كتبا كثيرة كأوّل **القانون** و**مختصر « المجسطى »** وكثيرا من الرسائل. ثمّ صنّف فى أرض الجبل

---

١) الشيخ أبو عبيد ا ب ج ن: أبو عبيد الجوزجانىّ صاحب الشيخ الرئيس ق/ص

٢) ههنا ا ب ج: هذا ن / / شاهدته أنا ا ج ن: سمعناه ب / / والله الموفّق ا ج ن: أو شاهدناه. + قيل إنّه كان وهو صبىّ من أجمل أهل زمانه وإنّ الناس كانوا فى يوم الجمعة يتراصّون فى الشوارع والطرق إذا خرج من دارهم إلى الجامع لينظروا إلى حسنه وجماله. ب

٤) فيها ا ب ج ن: بها ق/ص / / كنت ساقطة ق/ص

٥) كلّ ا ج ن: في كلّ ب / / فأقرأ ا ب ج ن: أقرأ ق/ص / / **المجسطى** ا ج ن ق/ص: من **المجسطى** عليه ب / / وأستملى ا ج ن ق/ص: وأستملى منه ب

٥–٦) فأملى علىّ **المختصر الأوسط** فى المنطق ساقطة ن

٨) أرض ا ب ج ق/ص: أوّل ن

Shaykh Abū ʿUbayd said:

This has been what the Master told me in his own words; from this point on I narrate the affairs of his which I witnessed. It is God who gives success.*

There was in Jurjān a man called Abū Muḥammad al-Shīrāzī,[54] who was an amateur of the sciences and who bought a house in his neighborhood for the Master to live in. I used | to attend him [Ibn Sīnā] every day and study the *Almagest* and ask for dictation in logic, so he dictated *The Middle Summary on Logic* to me and composed for Abū Muḥammad al-Shīrāzī *The Origin and the Return* and *Comprehensive Observations.* He wrote many works there, such as the first part of *The Qānūn* (*Canon*) [of medicine] and *Summary of the «Almagest»* and many treatises. The remaining works of his were written in the mountain country.[55]

* At this point B adds: It is said that when he was a young man he was one of the handsomest people of his time and that on Friday when he left his house to go to the mosque, the people used to crowd together in the streets and roads in order to catch a glimpse of his perfection and beauty.

باقى كتبه وهذا فهرست جميع كتبه:

(١) كتاب **المجموع** مجلّدة (٢) كتاب **الحاصل والمحصول** عشرون مجلّدة (٣) كتاب **البرّ والاثم** مجلّدتان (٤) كتاب **الشفاء** ثمانى عشرة مجلّدة (٥) كتاب **القانون** أربع عشرة مجلّدة (٦) كتاب **الارصاد الكلّيّة** مجلّدة (٧) كتاب **الانصاف** عشرون مجلّدة (٨) كتاب **النجاة** ثلاث مجلّدات (٩) كتاب **الهداية** مجلّدة (١٠) كتاب **الاشارات** مجلدة (١١) كتاب **المختصر الأوسط** مجلّدة (١٢) كتاب **العلائىّ** مجلّدة (١٣) كتاب **القولنج** مجلّدة (١٤) كتاب **لسان العرب** عشر مجلّدات (١٥) كتاب **الادوية القلبيّة** مجلّدة (١٦) كتاب **الموجز** مجلّدة (١٧) بعض **الحكمة المشرقيّة** مجلّدة (١٨) كتاب **بيان ذوات الجهة** مجلّدة (١٩) كتاب **المعاد** مجلّدة (٢٠) كتاب **المبدأ والمعاد** مجلّدة (٢١) كتاب **المباحثات** مجلّدة. ومن رسائله: (٢٢) رسالة **القضاء والقدر** (٢٣) **الآلة الرصديّة** (٢٤) **غرض قاطيغورياس** (٢٥) **المنطق** بالشعر (٢٦) **القصائد** فى العظمة والحكمة (٢٧) رسالة **في الحروف** (٢٨) **تعقّب المواضع الجدليّة** (٢٩) **مختصر أقليدس** (٣٠) **مختصر النبض**

---

١) باقى ا ب ج ن: باقية ق/ص // فهرست جميع كتبه] هذا الفهرست موجود فقط فى ق/ص

٦–٧) كتاب **الاشارات** . . . **العلائى** مجلّدة ساقطة ص

And here is a catalogue of all his books:[56]

[1] *The Compilation*, one volume; [2] *The Sum and Substance*, twenty volumes;[3] *Good Works and Evil*, two volumes;[4] *The Shifāʾ* (*Healing*), eighteen volumes;[5] *The Qānūn*, fourteen volumes; [6] *Comprehensive* | *Observations*, one volume; [7] *The Judgment*, twenty volumes; [8] *The Najāt* (*Deliverance*), three volumes; [9] *Guidance*, one volume; [10] *Instructions*, one volume; [11] *The Middle Summary*, one volume; [12] *The ʿAlāʾī*, one volume; [13] *The Colic*, one volume; [14] *The Arabic Language*, ten volumes; [15] *Cardiac Remedies*, one volume; [16] *The Epitome*, one volume; [17] | a portion of *The Eastern Philosophy*, one volume; [18] *Explanation of Modals*,[57] one volume; [19] *The Return*, one volume; [20] *The Origin and the Return;* [21] *Conversations*, one volume.

And among his treatises are [22] *Foreordination and Destiny;* [23] *Astronomical Instruments;* [24] *The Object of the "Categories";* [25] *Logic*, in poetic form; [26] *Poems on Majesty and Philosophy;* [27] *On the Consonants;* [28] | *Consideration of Dialectical Topics;* [29] *Summary of Euclid;* [30] *Summary on the Pulse*,

بالعجميـّة (٣١) **الحدود** (٣٢) **الأجرام السماويـّة** (٣٣) **الاشارة الى علم المنطق** (٣٤) **أقسام الحكمة** (٣٥) **النهاية واللانهاية** (٣٦) **عهد** كتبه لنفسه (٣٧) **حيّ بن يقظان** (٣٨) **في أنّ أبعاد الجسم غير ذاتيـّة له** (٣٩) **الكلام في الهندبا** وله خطبة (٤٠) **في أنه لا يجوز أن يكون شيء واحد جوهرا وعرضا** (٤١) **في أنّ علم زيد غير علم عمرو** (٤٢) رسائل له إخوانيـّة وسلطانيـّة (٤٣) رسائل فى مسائل جرت بينه وبين بعض الفضلاء (٤٤) كتاب **الحواشى على القانون** (٤٥) كتاب **عيون الحكمة** (٤٦) كتاب **الشبكة والطير** .

ثمّ انتقل إلى الريّ واتـّصل بخدمة السيـّدة وابنها[1] مجد الدولة . وعرفوه بسبب كتب وصلت معه تتضمـّن تعريف قدره . وكان بمجد

---

٢) النهاية ق: فى النهاية ص

٤) الكلام ق: خطب الكلام ص // وله خطبة ساقطة ص

٥) جوهرا وعرضا ق: جوهريـّا وعرضيـّا ص

٦) رسائل فى ساقطة ص

---

[1] سلطان الريّ

in Persian; [31] *Definitions;* [32] *Celestial Bodies;* [33] *Instruction in the Science of Logic;* [34] *The Branches of Philosophy;* [35] *Limit and Infinity;* [36] *A Testament*, which he made for himself; [37] *Ḥayy ibn Yaqẓān;* [38] *That the Dimensions of a Body are not Part of its Essence;* [39] *On Endive;* and his discourse [40] *On the | Impossibility of the Same Thing Being a Substance and an Accident;* [41] *That the Knowledge of Zayd is not the Knowledge of ᶜAmr;* [42] Letters to friends and officials; [43] Letters about questions which passed between him and other learned men; [44] *Comments on the "Qānūn";* [45] *Essential Philosophy;* [46] *The Net and the Bird.*

Then he moved to al-Rayy,[58] where he joined the service of al-Sayyida[59] and her son,* Majd al-Dawla.[60]|They learned of him through letters brought with him containing an appraisal of his worth. At that time Majd

* Sulṭān of al-Rayy.

الدولة إذ ذاك علّة السوداء. وصنّف هناك كتاب **المعاد** وأقام بها إلى أنّ قصدها شمس الدولة بعد قتل هلال بن بدر بن حسنويه وهزيمة عسكر بغداد. ثمّ اتّفقت له أسباب أوجبت خروجه إلى قزوين ومنها إلى همذان واتّصاله بخدمة كذبانويه والنظر في أسبابها.

ثمّ اتّفق معرفة شمس الدولة وإحضاره مجلسه بسبب قولنج كان قد أصابه. وعالجه حتّى شفاه الله وفاز من ذلك المجلس بخلع كثيرة. ورجع إلى داره بعد ما أقام هناك أربعين يوما بلياليها وصار من ندماء الأمير.

---

١) علّة ا ب ج: غلبة ن ق/ص / / السوداء] + فاشتغل بمداواته ق/ص: فاشتغل بمداواتها على هامش ج / / وصنّف ب ج ن ق/ص: فصنّف ا / / **المعاد**] + الأصغر على هامش ب

٢) بها ب ج ن ق/ص: به ا / / قصدها ا ب ج ن: قصد ق/ص / / بدر ب ج ن ق/ص: زيد ا

٣) له ساقطة ق/ص / / أوجبت خروجه ا ب ج ن: أوجبت الضرورة لها خروجه ق/ص

٤) كذبانويه ا ج ن ق/ص: كرمانويه ب ولكنّ كذبانويه على هامش ب

٦) اتّفق] + له ج

٧) ذلك ا ب ج ق/ص: تلك ن

al-Dawla had the illness of melancholia.* He wrote *The Return* there, and he remained there until Shams al-Dawla[62] attacked it, after the killing of Hilāl ibn Badr ibn Ḥasanūyah[63] and the rout of the troops of Baghdād. Then events occurred[64] which compelled him to depart for Qazwīn,[65] and from there to Hamadhān[66] where he joined the service of Kadhabānūyah[67] and managed | her business affairs.

Then he made the acquaintance of Shams al-Dawla, who summoned him to his court because of a colic which had afflicted him. He treated him until God cured him, and he obtained numerous robes of honor from that court. He returned to his house after staying there for forty days and nights, having become one of the companions of the Amīr.

---

* and so he set himself to treating it.[61]

ثمّ اتّفق نهوض الأمير إلى قرميسين لحرب عنّاز وخرج الشيخ فى خدمته . ثمّ توجّه نحو همذان منهزما راجعا ثمّ سألوه تقلّد الوزارة فتقلّدها ثمّ اتّفق تشويش العسكر عليه وإشفاقهم منه على أنفسهم . فكبسوا داره وأخذوه إلى الحبس وأغاروا على أسبابه وأخذوا جميع ما كان يملكه وساموا الأمير قتله . فامتنع من قتله وعدل إلى نفيه عن الدولة طلبا لمرضاتهم . فتوارى الشيخ فى دار الشيخ أبى سعد بن دخدول أربعين يوما . فعاود القولنج للأمير شمس الدولة وطلب الشيخ فحضر مجلسه . واعتذر الأمير إليه بكلّ الاعتذار فاشتغل بمعالجته . وأقام عنده مكرّما مبجّلا وأُعيدت الوزارة إليه ثانياً .

---

١) إلى ساقطة ا / / عنّاز ا ب ن ق/ص : عباد ج

٣) اتّفق ساقطة ب ولكنّها على الهامش

٦) من قتله ا ب ج : عن قتله ن : منه ق/ص / / عن الدولة ا ب ج ق/ص : من المملكة ن / / الشيخ ساقطة ق/ص

٧) الشيخ ساقطة ن / / سعد ا ج ن ق/ص : سعيد ب / / دخدول ا ب ج : دخدوك ن ق/ص

٨) القولنج للأمير شمس الدولة ا ب ج ن (الأمير ن) : الأمير شمس الدولة علّة القولنج ق/ص (علّة ساقطة ص) / / واعتذر ا ج ن : فاعتذر ب

Then the Amīr went up to Qirmīsīn[68] to make war on ʿAnnāz,[69] with the Master riding out in his service. He fell back in flight toward Hamadhān, and they [the court] asked him to take over the vizierate, which he did, but the troops mutinied against him, being apprehensive about their positions on account of him. So they surrounded his house, took him off to prison, ransacked | his goods, took everything he owned, and even demanded his execution by the Amīr. He refused to execute him, but compromised by banishing him from the state, since he desired to satisfy them. And so the Master concealed himself in the house of Shaykh Abū Saʿd ibn Dakhdūl[70] for forty days; but the colic seized Amīr Shams al-Dawla again, and he sent for the Master, who came to his court. The Amīr apologized to him profusely, and he devoted himself to treating him. And so he remained with him, honored and revered, | and the vizierate was given back to him a second time.

ثمّ سألته أنا شرح كتب أرسطو فذكر أنّه لا فراغ له إلى ذلك فى ذلك الوقت . « ولكن إن رضيت منّى بتصنيف كتاب أورد فيه ما صحّ عندى من هذه العلوم بلا مناظرة مع المخالفين ولا الاشتغال بالردّ عليهم فعلت ذلك. » فرضيت به فابتدأ بالطبيعيّات من كتاب سمّاه كتاب **الشفاء**. وكان قد صنّف الكتاب الأوّل من **القانون** وكان يجتمع كلّ ليلة فى داره طلبة العلم وكنت أقرأ من **الشفاء** نوبة وكان يقرأ غيرى من **القانون** نوبة . فإذا فرغنا حضر المغنّون على اختلاف طبقاتهم وعبّى مجلس الشراب بآلاته وكنّا نشتغل به . وكان التدريس بالليل لعدم الفراغ بالنهار

---

١) أرسطو ا ب ج: أرسطو طاليس ن ق/ص / / فذكر] + له ا

٢) فى ذلك ساقطة ج ولكنّها على الهامش

٤) الاشتغال ا ب ج ن: اشتغال ق/ص / / فرضيت ا ب ن ق/ص: ورضيت ج / / فابتدأ ج ن ق/ص: فابتدأنا ا ب / / بالطبيعيّات ساقطة ب ولكنّها على الهامش

٦) وكان ج ق/ص: فكان ا ب ن / / يجتمع ان ق/ص: يجمع ب ج

٧) يقرأ غيرى ا ج ن ق/ص: غيرى يقرأ ب / / فرغنا ب ج ن ق/ص: حضرنا ا

٨) وعبّى ا ب: وهبّىء ج ن

٩) وكان ساقطة ا ولكنّها فوق الخطّ

Then I asked him to comment on the works of Aristotle, but he said that he was not free to do so at that time. "But if you would be satisfied with my composing a work in which I would set forth what, to me, is sound in these sciences, without debating with those who disagree or devoting myself to their refutation, I would do that." I was satisfied with it and so he began with the "Physics" | of a work which he called the *Shifāʾ* (*Healing*). He had already written the first book of the *Qānūn*, and every night pupils would gather at his house, while by turns I would read from the *Shifāʾ* and someone else would read from the *Qānūn*.[71] When we were finished, different kinds of singers appeared, a drinking party was prepared with its utensils, and we partook of it. The instruction took place at night, because of the lack of free time during the day

خدمة للأمير .

فقضينا على ذلك زمنا ثمّ توجّه شمس الدولة إلى الطارم لحرب أميرها . وعاوده القولنج فى قرب ذلك الموضع واشتدّت علّة وانضاف إليه أمراض أخر جبلها سؤ تدبيره وقلّة قبوله من الشيخ. فخاف العسكر وفاته فرجعوا به طالبين همذان فى المهد فتُوُفّى في الطريق . ثمّ بُوْيِـع[1] ابن شمس الدولة وطلبوا استيزار الشيخ. فأبى عليهم وكاتب علاء الدولة يطلب خدمته سرّا والمصير إليه والانضمام إلى جانبه .

وأقام فى دار أبى غالب العطّار متواريا وطلبت منه إتمام

---

١) خدمة للأمير ا ج ن ق/ص : بخدمة الأمير ب

٢) الطارم ا ب ج ن: طارم ق/ص

٣) أميرها ا ب ن: الأمير ج + بهاء الدولة فوق الخطّ: الأمير بها ق/ص

٤) إليه ا ب ج ن: إلى ذلك ق/ص / / جبلها ج ن ق/ص وعلى هامش ب: حملتها ا ب / / قبوله ا ب ج ن: القبول ق/ص

٥) المهد ب ج ن ق/ص: المهر ا

٧) وكاتب ا ب ن ق/ص: وكان ج / / يطلب خدمته سرّا ا ب ج ن: سرّا يطلب خدمته ق/ص

---

[1] علىّ

on account of his service to the Amīr.

After we had spent some time at this, Shams al-Dawla set out for al-Ṭārum[72] to make war on its Amīr.[73] He was attacked again by the colic in the vicinity of that place and his illness became more severe, adding to which were other ailments which his not taking care of himself and seldom accepting | the Master's orders caused. The troops feared his death, so they returned, setting out for Hamadhān with him in a litter, but he died on the way. The son* of Shams al-Dawla[74] was then acknowledged as sovereign and they [the court] asked that the Master be appointed vizier. But he turned them down and corresponded with ʿAlāʾ al-Dawla[75] in secret, desiring to serve him, cast his lot with him, and to join his court.

He remained in hiding in the house of Abū Ghālib the Druggist,[76] where I asked him to finish

* ʿAlī ibn Shams al-Dawla.

كتاب **الشفاء** فاستحضر أبا غالب وطلب منه الكاغد والمحبرة فأحضرهما. وكتب الشيخ فى قريب من عشرين جزءا مقدار الثمن رؤوس المسائل. وبقى فيه يومين حتّى كتب رؤوس المسائل بلا كتاب يحضره ولا أصل يرجع إليه . بل من حفظه وعن ظهر قابه. ثمّ ترك تلك الأجزاء بين يديه وأخذ الكاغد فكان ينظر فى كلّ مسألة ويكتب شرحها. فكان يكتب كلّ يوم خمسين ورقة حتّى أتى على جميع الطبيعيّات والإلهيّات ما خلا كتاب الحيوان. وابتدأ بالمنطق وكتب منه جزءا . ثمّ اتّهمه تاج الملك بمكاتبته علاء الدولة وأنكر عليه ذلك وحثّ فى طلبه. فدلّ عليه بعض أعدائه فأخذوه

---

١) منه ساقطة ق/ص / / والمحبرة ا ب ج ق/ص: والمحبر ن

٢) من ساقطة ان : مقدار الثمن ا ب ج ن: على الثمن بخطّه ق/ص

٣) رؤوس المسائل] + كلّها ن ق/ص وعلى هامش ج

٤) عن ساقطة ن

٦) كلّ ا ج ن ق/ص: فى كلّ ب / / حتّى أتى ا ب ج ق/ص: وأتى ن

٧) كتاب ا ب ج ن: كتابى ق/ص / / الحيوان] + والنبات ق/ص وعلى هامش ج

٨) بمكاتبته ج ق/ص: بمكاتبة ا ب ن / / وأنكر ا ب ج ن: فأنكر ق/ص

٩) فى طلبه ا ب ن ق/ص: على طلبه ج

the *Shifāʾ;* he sent for Abū Ghālib and asked him for paper and an inkstand, which he brought. The Master wrote down the main topics in approximately twenty quires of one-eighth [octavo?] size, continuing on it for two days, until he had written down the main topics without the presence of a book or source to consult, but entirely from his memory and by heart. Then | he placed these quires before him, took a sheet of paper, examined each problem and wrote a commentary on it. He would write fifty pages every day, until he had finished all of the "Physics" and "Metaphysics," with the exception of the book on Animals.[77] He then began on the "Logic" and wrote one section of it; at that point Tāj al-Mulk[78] became suspicious of him over his corresponding with ʿAlāʾ al-Dawla, became angry at him for doing so, and consequently instigated a search for him. Some one of his enemies informed on him; they seized him

وحملوه إلى قلعة يقال لها فردجان. وأنشد هناك قصيدة فيها:

دخولى فى اليقين كما تراه وكلّ الشكّ فى أمر الخروج

وبقى فيها أربعة أشهر ثمّ قصد علاء الدولة همذان فأخذها. وانهزم تاج الملك ومرّ إلى تلك القلعة بعينها. ثمّ رجع علاء الدولة عن همذان وعاد تاج الملك بن شمس الدولة إلى همذان واستصحب الشيخ معه. ونزل فى دار العلوىّ واشتغل بتنصيف المنطق من كتاب **الشفاء**. وكان قد صنّف بالقلعة كتاب **الهداية** ورسالة **حىّ بن يقظان** وكتاب **القولنج** وأمّا **الادوية القلبية** فإنمّا صنفّها

---

١) حملوه ا ب ج ن: أدّوه ق/ص / / فردجان ان ق/ص: فرودخان ب: نردوان على هامش ب: مزدوان ج / / وأنشد ا ب ج ن: وأنشأ ق/ص / / فيها ا ب: منها ج ن

٢) فى اليقين ا ب ج: باليقين ن ق/ص

٣) همذان ان ق/ص وعلى هامش ب: بهملان ب: عن همذان ج / / فأخذها ا ب ج ن: وأخذها ق/ص

٥) عن ساقطة ج ولكنّها على الهامش / / بن شمس الدولة ا ج ن: ساقطة ب ولكنّها على الهامش: وابن شمس الدولة ق/ص: و ا فوق خطّ ج

٦) واستصحب الشيخ معه ا ب ج ن: وحملوا معهم الشيخ إلى همذان ق/ص / / واشتغل] + هناك ق/ص

٨) أمّا فوق خطّ ا / / فانـّما ان ق/ص: فانـّه ب: فانـّها ج

and took him to a castle which is called Fardajān.[79] There he recited an ode in which is [found the following verse]:

As you can see, my going in's a certainty,
And all the doubt is on the point of getting out.

He remained there four months, until ʿAlāʾ al-Dawla attacked Hamadhān and seized it.[80] Tāj al-Mulk was routed and moved into this very same castle. When ʿAlāʾ | al-Dawla withdrew from Hamadhān, Tāj al-Mulk, the son of Shams al-Dawla,[81] returned to Hamadhān and took the Master along with him. He stayed in the house of the ʿAlid[82] and occupied himself with writing the "Logic" of the *Shifāʾ*. In the castle he had written *Guidance* and *Ḥayy ibn Yaqẓān* (*Alive, the Son of Awake*) and *The Colic; Cardiac Remedies* he composed, on the other hand,

أوّل وروده إلى همذان.

وكان تقضّى على هذا زمان وتاج الملك فى أثناء هذا يمنّية بمواعيد جميلة. ثمّ عزم الشيخ على التوجّه إلى إصفهان فخرج متنكّرا وأنا معه وأخوه وغلامان فى زىّ الصوفيّة إلى أن وصلنا إلى طهران على باب إصفهان بعد أن قاسينا شدائد فى الطريق. فاستقبلنا أصدقاء الشيخ وندماء الأمير علاء الدولة وخواصّه وحمل إليه الثياب والمراكب الخاصّة. وأنزل فى محلّة يقال لها كوى كنبذ فى دار عبد الله بن بيبى وفيها من الآلات والفرش ما

---

١) إلى ساقطة ج ن

٢) تقضّى ب ن ق/ص: يقضى ا : يمضى ج // زمان ب ن ق/ص: زمانا ا: أزمان ج

٣) عزم الشيخ على ا ب ج ن: عنّ للشيخ ق/ص

٤) وأنا معه وأخوه وغلامان ا ب ج: وأنا معه وأخوه ن: وأنا وأخوه وغلامان معه ق/ص

٥) طهران ج: طبران ا ب ن ق/ص

٧) المراكب ا ج ن ق/ص: المواكب ب

٧–٨) كوى كنبذ ج: كون كنبذا ب ن ق/ص

٨) بيبى ا ب ج: بابى ن ق/ص

right after his arrival in Hamadhān.

He had spent some time on this, and all this while Tāj al-Mulk was tempting him with handsome promises, when the Master then decided to set out for Iṣfahān,[83] and so he left, I with him, along with his brother and two slaves, disguised in the dress of Ṣūfism, travelling until we reached | Ṭihrān,[84] at the gate of Iṣfahān, after we had suffered hardships on the way. Friends of the Master and the companions and courtiers of Amīr ᶜAlāʾ al-Dawla met us, and clothing and special mounts were brought to him. He was lodged in a quarter called Kūy Kunbādh[85] in the house of ᶜAbd Allāh ibn Bībī,[86] which contained all the utensils and furnishings which

يحتاج إليه. فصادف من مجلسه الإكرام والإعزاز الّذى يستحقّه مثله. ثمّ رسم الأمير علاء الدولة ليالى الجمعات مجلس النظر بين يديه فحضره سائر العلماء على اختلاف طبقاتهم والشيخ فى جملتهم فما كان يُطاق فى شىء من العلوم.

واشتغل بإصفهان بتتميم كتاب **الشفاء** ففرغ من المنطق والمجسطى وكان قد اختصر أوقليدس والأرثماطيقى والموسيقى . وأورد فى كلّ كتاب من الرياضيّات زيادات رأى أنّ الحاجة إليها داعية. أمّا فى المجسطى فأورد عشرة أشكال فى اختلاف المنظر. وأورد فى آخر المجسطى فى علم الهيئة أشياء لم يسبق إليها. وأورد فى

---

١) فصادف ا ق/ص: وصادف ب ج: وصادفه ن / / من ا ب ج ن: فى ق/ص

٢) مثله ساقطة ب / / الأمير ساقطة ب / / ليالى ا ج ن ق/ص: ان ليالى ب / / الجمعات ج ن ق/ص وعلى هامش ب: الجماعات ا ب

٣) فحضره ا ب ج ن: بحضرة ق/ص / / فى ا ب ج ن: من ق/ص

٤) فما كان يطاق ا ب ن ق/ص: ممّا كان لا يطاق ج

٥) بتتميم ب ج ن ق/ص: بينهم ا

٨) أشكال ساقطة ا

٩) فى علم ا ب ج ق/ص: من ن

he needed. And from his court he received the respect and esteem which someone like him deserved. Amīr ʿAlāʾ al-Dawla designated Friday nights for learned discussions in his presence, which all of the different classes of learned men attended, the Master among them, and he was not outclassed in any of the sciences. |

He occupied himself in Iṣfahān with finishing the *Shifāʾ*, completing the "Logic" and the Almagest, since he had already summarized Euclid,[87] the Arithmetic, and the Music. In every book of the "Mathematics" he presented additional materials, the need for which he thought to be compelling; as for the Almagest, he presented ten figures illustrating parallax. And elsewhere in the Almagest on the science of astronomy, he presented materials which were unprecedented. In Euclid he presented

أوقليدس شبهاء وفى الأرثماطيقى خواصّ حسنة وفى الموسيقى مسائل غفل عنها الأوّلون. وتمّ كتاب **الشفاء** ما خلا كتابى النبات والحيوان فإنّه صنّفها فى السنة الّتى توجّه فيها علاء الدولة إلى سابور خواست فى الطريق. وصنّف أيضا فى الطريق كتاب **النجاة**.

واختصّ بعلاء الدولة وصار من ندمائه إلى أن عزم علاء الدولة على قصد همذان وخرج الشيخ فى الصحبة. فجرى ليلة بين يدى علاء الدولة ذكر الخلل الحاصل فى التقاويم المعمولة بحسب الأرصاد القديمة فأمر الأمير الشيخ بالاشتغال برصد هذه الكواكب وأطلق من الأموال ما يحتاج إليه. وابتدأ الشيخ به وولّانى اتّخاذ آلاتها واستخدام صنّاعها. حتّى ظهر كثير من المسائل. وكان

---

١) شبهاء : شبها فى كلّ النصوص / / خواصّ ب ن ق/ص : خواصّا ا ج

٢) الأوّلون ا جن ق/ص : الأوائل ب / / كتاب **الشفاء** ا ب جن : الكتاب المعروف بالشفاء ق/ص / / كتابى ن ق/ص : كتاب ا ب ج

٣) فيها ا ب ن ق/ص : فيه ج / / إلى ساقطة ج ولكنّها على الهامش

٣–٦) إلى سابور خواست . . . الدولة ساقطة ب ولكنها على الهامش

٨) الأرصاد القديمة ا ج ن ق/ص : الأرصاد الكلّيّة القديمة ب / / بالاشتغال ا ج : الاشتغال ب : ساقطة ن

some geometrical figures,[88] in the Arithmetic some excellent numerical properties, and in the Music some problems which the ancients had neglected. Thus he finished the *Shifāʾ*, except for the two books on the Plants and the Animals, which he wrote on the way in the year that ʿAlāʾ al-Dawla attacked Sābūr Khwāst.[89] He also wrote the *Najāt* en route. |

He was made a member of the court by ʿAlāʾ al-Dawla and became one of his companions, to the point that when ʿAlāʾ al-Dawla decided to attack Hamadhān the Master accompanied him. One night in the presence of ʿAlāʾ al-Dawla someone mentioned the discrepancies contained in the ephemerides compiled on the basis of the ancient astronomical observations, and so the Amīr ordered the Master to devote himself to the observation of these stars, and he allocated whatever funds he needed. The Master set about it and charged me | with obtaining the required instruments and hiring those skilled in making them, so that many of the problems came to light.

يقع الخلل فى أمر الرصد لكثرة الأسفار وعوائقها.

وصنّف الشيخ بإصفهان **الكتاب العلائى**. وكان من عجائب الشيخ أنّى صحبته وخدمته خمسا وعشرين سنة فما رأيته إذا وقع له كتاب مجدّد ينظر فيه على الولاء. بل كان يقصد المواضع الصعبة منه والمسائل المشكلة فينظر ما قاله مصنّفه فيها. فيتبيّن مرتبته فى العلم ودرجته فى الفهم.

وكان الشيخ جالسا يوما بين يدى الأمير وأبو منصور الجبّان حاضر. فجرى فى اللغة مسألة تكلّم الشيخ فيها بما حضره فالتفت أبو منصور إلى الشيخ وقال « أنت فيلسوف وحكيم ولكن لم تقرأ

---

١) الرصد ا ب ج ق/ص: الأرصاد ن

٢) **الكتاب** ا ب ج: **كتاب** ن / / عجائب الشيخ ب ج ن: عجاب الشيخ ا: عجائب أمر الشيخ ق/ص

٣) صحبته و ساقطة ن / / خمسا ن ق/ص: خمسة ا ب ج

٤) مجدّد ا ب ن ق/ص: جديد ج

٧) يوما ا ب ج ن: يوما من الأيّام ق/ص / / الجبّان ا ب ج: الجبّائى ن

٨) حاضر ان ق/ص: حاضرا ب: ساقطة ج ولكنها على الهامش / / الشيخ فيها ا ج ن ق/ص: فيها الشيخ ب

٩) وقال «أنت ا ج: وقال له «أنت ب ن: يقول إنّك ق/ص / / لم ساقطة ا / / تقرأ ا ب ج ق/ص: تفز ن

The discrepancies in the matter of observation had occurred because of the great number of journeys and the attendant errors.[90]

The Master wrote the *ʿAlāʾī*[91] in Iṣfahān as well. One of the remarkable things about the Master was that for the twenty-five years[92] that I was his companion and servant, I did not once see him, when he came across a new book, examine it from beginning to end. Rather he would go directly to its difficult passages | and intricate problems and look at what its author had to say about them. Thus would he seek to ascertain the level of his knowledge and the degree of his understanding.

One day the Master was sitting in the presence of the Amīr while Abū Manṣūr al-Jabbān[93] was present. A question concerning philology was raised, and the Master had spoken his thoughts in the matter when Abū Manṣūr turned to the Master and said, "You are a philosopher and a physician, but you have not studied

من اللغة ما يُـرضَى كلامك فيها.» فاستنكف الشيخ من هذا الكلام وتوفّر على درس كتب اللغة ثلاث سنين واستدعى بكتاب **تهذيب اللغة** من خراسان من تصنيف أبى منصور الأزهريّ. فبلغ الشيخ فى اللغة طبقة قلّما يتّفق مثلها.

وأنشد ثلاث قصائد ضمّنها ألفاظا غريبة في اللغة وكتب ثلاثة كتب أحدها على طريقة ابن العميد والآخر على طريقة الصابيّ والآخر على طريقة الصاحب. وأمر بتجليدها وإخلاق جلدها. ثمّ أوعز إلى الأمير بعرض تلك المجلّدة على أبى منصور الجبّان وذكر «إنّا ظفرنا بهذه المجلّدة في الصحراء وقت الصيد فيجب أن تتفقّدها وتقول لنا ما فيها.» فنظر فيها أبو منصور وأشكل عليه كثير ممّا فيها. فقال له الشيخ «إنّ ما تجهله من هذا الكتاب

---

١) من اللغة ا ج ن ق/ص: فى اللغة ب / / يرضى ا ب ج ق/ص: نرضى ن

٥) وأنشد ا ب ج ن: وأنشأ ق/ص / / ألفاظا] + ألفاظا ب (مرّة ثانية) / / ثلاثة ن ق/ص: ثلاث ا ب ج

٨) إلى ساقطة ا ج ن ق/ص

١٠) أبو منصور] + الجبّان ب

١١) إنّ ساقطة ن

enough philology so that your remarks on it should be accepted." The Master became incensed at this remark and devoted himself to an intensive study of books on philology for three years, even sending to Khurāsān for the *Correct Philology*, one of the works of Abū Manṣūr al-Azharī.[94] And so in philology the Master reached a stage the like of which seldom occurs. |

He wrote three odes in which he included words rare in the language, and he wrote three letters, the first of which was in the style of Ibn al-ᶜAmīd,[95] another in the style of al-Ṣābī,[96] and the last in the style of al-Ṣāḥib.[97] He ordered them to be bound and their leather made to look worn. He then asked the Amīr to present this volume to Abū Manṣūr al-Jabbān while saying, "We came into possession of this book while hunting in the desert; you must | examine it and tell us what it contains." And so Abū Manṣūr examined it carefully, and much of what was in it was difficult for him. So the Master said to him, "Whatever material in this book is incomprehensible to you

فهو مذكور فى الموضع الفلانىّ من كتب اللغة» وذكر له كتبا معروفة في اللغة كان الشيخ قد حفظ تلك الألفاظ منها. وكان أبو منصور مخرّفا فيما يورده من اللغة غير ثقة فيها ففطن أنّ تلك الرسائل من تصنيف الشيخ وأنّ الّذى حمله عليه ما جبهه به ذلك اليوم فتنصّل واعتذر إليه. ثمّ صنّف الشيخ كتابا فى اللغة سمّاه **لسان العرب** لم يُصَنَّف فى اللغة مثله ولم ينقله إلى البياض . ثمّ توفّى وبقى الكتاب على مسوّدته لا يهتدى أحد إلى ترتيبه .

وكان قد حصّل تجارب كثيرة فيما باشره من المعالجات وعزم

---

١) فى الموضع الفلانىّ ا ن ق/ص: فى الكتاب فى الموضع الفلانىّ ب: فى الكتاب الفلانىّ ج

٣) مخرّفا ب: محزفا ا: محرّفا ج: مجزفا ن ق/ص / / ففطن] + أبو منصور ق/ص

٥) ذلك اليوم ا ب ج ن: فى ذلك اليوم ق/ص / / إليه ا ب ن ق/ص: له ج

٧) ثمّ ا ب ج ن: حتّى ق/ص / / وبقى ا ب ج ن: فبقى ق/ص / /الكتاب ساقطة ق/ص

٩) حصّل] + له ج: + للشيخ ق/ص / / باشره ج ق/ص: باشر ا ب ن / / وعزم ا ب ج ن: عزم ق/ص

is mentioned in such-and-such a place in one of the books on philology," mentioning to him well-known books in philology, from which the Master had memorized those passages. Abū Manṣūr had been prattling in the philology he had put forward, without authority to back it up; so then he realized that these letters were written by the Master, and that his insulting him | that day was what brought it upon him. So he cleared himself by apologizing to him. The Master then wrote a book on philology which he called *The Arabic Language*, which has not been equaled in philology, but he did not transcribe it into clean copy. The writing was still in its rough state when he died, and no one could discover how to put it in order.

He carried out many experiments in his medical practice which he decided

على تدوينها فى كتاب **القانون**. وكان قد علّقها على أجزاء فضاعت قبل تمام كتاب **القانون**. من ذلك أنّه تصدّع يوما فتصوّر أنّ مادّة تريد النزول إلى حجاب رأسه وأنّه لا يأمن ورما يحصل فيه. فأمر بإحضار ثلج كثير ودقّه ولفّه فى خرقة وغطّى بها رأسه. وفعل ذلك حتّى قَوِيَ الموضع وامتنع عن قبول تلك المادّة وعوفى. ومن ذلك أنّ امرأة مسلولة بخوارزم أمرها أن لا تتناول شيئا من الأدوية سوى جلنجبين السكّر حتّى تناولت على الأيّام مقدار مائة منّ وشُفِيَت.

وكان الشيخ قد صنّف بجرجان **المختصر الأصغر في المنطق** وهو

١–٢) وكان . . . **القانون** ساقطة ن

٢) تمام ا ج ق/ص : اتمام ب // كتاب **القانون** ا ب ق/ص : الكتاب ج // تصدّع ب ج ن: تصرّع ا : صدّع ق/ص // يوما ا ب ج ق/ص : مرّة ن

٤) وغطّى بها رأسه ج ن : وغطّى به رأسه ا ب : وتغتية رأسه بها ق/ص

٥) حتّى ب ج ن ق/ص : حقّ ا // قبول ا ب ج ق/ص : حلول ن

٦) أنّ ساقطة ا ب

٧) جلنجبين ج ن ق/ص وعلى هامشى ا ب : سكنجبين ا ب

٨) وشفيت] + المرأة ق/ص

٩) وهو ساقطة ب

to record in the *Qānūn*. He had jotted them down in some quires, but they were lost before the completion of the *Qānūn*. For example, one day when he had a headache, he imagined that a substance was trying to descend to the membrane of his skull and he felt uneasy about a swelling which might occur there, so he ordered a large supply of ice to be brought; he crushed it and wrapped it in a cloth, with which he covered his head. | He continued doing this until he overcame the area [of swelling], and prevented the reception of this substance, and so was cured. Another example is that of a tubercular woman in Khwārazm whom he ordered to take no medicine other than rose preserve made with sugar,[98] until, in the course of time, she had taken one hundred *manns*,[99] and was cured.

The Master had written *The Shorter Summary on Logic* in Jurjān, and it was

الّذى وضعه بعد ذلك فى أوّل **النجاة**. ووقعت نسخته إلى شيراز فنظر فيها جماعة من أهل العلم هناك. فوقعت لهم الشبه فى مسائل منها وكتبوها على جزء. وكان القاضى بشيراز من جملة القوم فأنفذ بالجزء إلى أبى القاسم الكرمانىّ صاحب إبراهيم بن بابا الديلمىّ المشتغل بعلم الباطن وأضاف إليه كتابا إلى الشيخ أبى القاسم. وأنفذهما مع ركابىّ قاصد وسأله عرض الجزء على الشيخ وتنجّز جوابه فيه. فحضر الشيخ أبو القاسم فى يوم صائف عند اصفرار الشمس عند الشيخ وعرض عليه الكتاب والجزء. فقرأ

---

١) نسخته ا ب ج ن: نسخة ق/ص

٢) فنظر ا ب ج ق/ص: ونظر ن // فيها] + فنظر فيها (مرّة ثانية) // هناك ساقطة ب // الشبه ق/ص: الشبه فيها ب: الشبهة ا ج ن

٣) وكتبوها ا ب ج ن: فكتبوها ق ص

٤) بالجزء ا ب ق/ص: الجزء ج ن

٥) الباطن ا ج ن: المنطق والباطن ب // وأضاف ا ج ق/ص: فأضاف ب ن // الشيخ ساقطة ن

٦) مع ا ب ج ن: على يدى ق/ص

٧) جوابه ا ب ج ن: أجوبته ق/ص // يوم ساقطة ن // صائف ا ب ن: صارف ج

٧–٨) فحضر . . . الشيخ ا ب ج ن: وإذا الشيخ أبو القاسم دخل على الشيخ عند اصفرار الشمس فى يوم صائف ق/ص

that which he included in the first part of the *Najāt* afterwards. A copy of it arrived in Shīrāz[100] and a group of the learned men there examined it. They had doubts about some problems in it, so they wrote them down in a quire. The Qāḍī of Shīrāz was one of this group of people, so he sent the quire to Abū al-Qāsim al-Kirmānī,[101] a friend of Ibrāhīm ibn | Bābā al-Daylamī,[102] a devotee of the science of esoteric interpretation,[103] and he added to it a letter to Shaykh Abū al-Qāsim. He sent them both with an express courier and asked that he present the quire to the Master and request a reply from him concerning it. So one warm day as the sun was paling, Shaykh Abū al-Qāsim came to the Master's house and presented the letter and the quire to him. He read

الكتاب وردّه عليه وترك الجزء بين يديه والناس يتحدّثون وهو ينظر فيه . ثمّ خرج أبو القاسم وأمرنى الشيخ بإحضار البياض فشددت له خمسة أجزاء كلّ واحد عشرة أوراق بالربع الفرعونىّ . وصلّينا العشاء وقدّم الشمع وأمر بإحضار الشراب. وأجلسنى وأخاه وأمرنا بتناول الشراب وابتدأ هو بجواب تلك المسائل . وكان يكتب ويشرب إلى نصف الليل حتّى غلبنى وأخاه النوم فأمرنا بالانصراف. وعند الصباح حضر رسوله يستحضرنى فحضرت وهو على المصلّى. وبين يديه الأجزاء الخمسة. فقال «خذها وصر بها إلى الشيخ أبى القاسم الكرمانىّ وقل له استعجلت فى الإجابة

١–٢) والناس . . . فيه ا ب ج ن: وهو ينظر فيه والناس يتحدّثون ق/ص

٢) البياض] + وقطع أجزاء منه ق/ص

٣) فشددت ا ب ج ق/ص: فعددت ن // عشرة ا ج ن ق/ص: عشر ب

٤) وأمر ا ب ج: وأمرنا ن

٥) وابتدأ هو ا ج ن ق/ص: وأقبل هو وابتدأ ب

٧) وعند ا ب ج ن: فعند ق/ص // حضر رسوله ا ب ج ن: قرع الباب فاذا رسول الشيخ ق/ص // فحضرت ا ب ج: بحضرته ن: فحضرته ق/ص

٨) فقال ا ب ج ق/ص: وقال ن // صر ب ج ن ق/ص: مر ا

٩) الإجابة ا ب ن: الجواب ج

the letter and returned it to him, placed the quire before him, and examined it while the people around were chatting. As soon as Abū al-Qāsim left, the Master ordered me to bring blank paper, so I sewed five quires for him, each one of ten sheets of Firʿawnī[104] quarto. After we prayed the evening prayer, he set out candles and ordered wine to be brought. He asked his brother and me to sit down | and asked us to have some wine while he began replying to these problems. He wrote and drank until the middle of the night, at which time sleep overcame his brother and me, and he asked us to leave. In the morning his messenger appeared, summoning me, so I presented myself while he was at prayer. Before him were the five quires. He said, "Take these and deliver them to Abū al-Qāsim al-Kirmānī and tell him I was in a hurry to answer

عنها لئلاّ يتعوّق الركابىّ.» فلمّا حملتها تعجّب كلّ العجب وصرف الفيج وأعلمهم بهذه الحالة وصار الحديث تأريخا بين الناس.

ووضع فى حال الرصد آلات ما سُبِق إليها وصنّف فيها رسالة. وبقيت أنا ثمانى سنين مشغولا بالرصد وكان غرضى تبيين ما يحكيه بطلميوس فى أرصاده. وصنّف الشيخ كتاب **الانصاف** واليوم الّذى قدم فيه السلطان مسعود إصفهان نهب عسكره رحل الشيخ وكان الكتاب فى جملته وما وقف له على أثر.

وكان الشيخ قوىّ القوى كلّها وقوّة المجامعة من قواه

---

١) حملتها ا ب ج ن: حملته إليه ق/ص

٢) الحالة ساقطة ن / / الحديث ا ب ج ن: هذا الحديث ق/ص

٣) حال ا ج ن ق /ص: حالات ب

٤) ثمانى ب: ثمان ا ج ن

٥) ما يحكيه فوق خطّ ا / / بطلميوس ب ق/ص: بطليموس ا ج ن / / فى أرصاده ا ب ج ن: عن نفسه (قصّته ص) فى الأرصاد حتّى بان (فتبيّن ص) لى بعضها ق/ص / / الشيخ ساقطة ب

٦) قدم ا ب ج ق/ص: قصد ن / / إصفهان ا ب ج ن: إلى إصفهان ق/ص

٧) وما ا ب ن ق/ص: ما ج / / وقف] + بعد ذلك على هامش ج

٨) وقوّة ا ب ج ن: وكانت قوّة ق/ص

them so that the messenger might not be delayed." When I delivered them, he was greatly astonished; he sent back the messenger and informed them about this matter, and so the story became historic among the people.

In the course of his astronomical observations, he invented instruments which had never before existed and wrote a treatise about them. For eight years I remained occupied with observation, my goal being to explain | what Ptolemy had reported concerning his observations. The Master also wrote *The Judgment*, but on the day when Sulṭān Masʿūd[105] arrived at Iṣfahān, his troops rifled the Master's baggage which contained the work and it was not found afterwards.[106]

The Master was vigorous in all his faculties, the sexual faculty being the most vigorous and dominant of his

الشهوانيّة أقوى وأغلب ويشتغل به كثيرا. فأثّر فى مزاجه وكان يعتمد على قوّة مزاجه حتّى صار أمره فى السنة التّى حارب فيها علاء الدولة تاش فرّاش على باب الكرج أصاب الشيخ قولنج. ولحرصه على البرء إشفاقا من هزيمة يدفع إليها لا يتأتّى له المسير فيها مع المرض، حقن نفسه فى يوم واحد ثمانى مرّات فتقرّح بعض أمعائه وظهر به سحج. وأُحْوِجَ إلى المسير مع علاء الدولة بسرعة نحو إيذج فظهر به هناك الصرع الّذى قد يتبع

---

١) ويشتغل به كثيراً ا ج ن: ويشتغل فيه كثيراً ب: وكان كثيراً ما يشتغل به ق/ص كثيرا] + فقيل له فيه وفى كثرة المأكول والسهر فقال «إنّ الله تعالى قد وفّر فى قواى الظاهرة والباطنة فانا أوفى كلّ قوّة حقّها.» ب / / وكان] + الشيخ ق/ص

٣) الكرج ب ج: الكرخ ان ق/ص / / أصاب ا ب ج ن: إلى أن أخذ ق/ص / / قولنج ب ق/ص: القولنج ا ج ن

٤) البرء ا ب ج ن: برئه ق/ص / / إشفاقا ن ق/ص: اسفا ا: وإشفاقه ب: وإشفاقا ج / / لا ب ج: الا ا: ولا ن ق/ص

٥) واحد ساقطة ج ولكنّها على الهامش / / ثمانى ب: ثمان ا ج ن

٦) وأحوج ب ج ن ق/ص: وحوج ا

٧) إيذج ن ق/ص: ايلح ا: بلح ب: ابرح ج / / بسرعة نحو . . . ا ب ج: نحو أيذج بسرعة ن: فأسرعوا نحو إيذج ق/ص / / فظهر ا ب ن ق/ص: وظهر ج / / قد ساقطة ن

concupiscible faculties,[107] and he exercised it often.* It affected his constitution, upon whose strength he depended, to the point that in the year in which ʿAlāʾ al-Dawla fought against Tāsh Farrāsh[108] at the gate of al-Karaj,[109] the Master was afflicted by the colic. He desired to recover at once because of his concern over a retreat to which he [ʿAlāʾ al-Dawla] might be driven, in which case | the march could not be undertaken by him on account of his illness. Therefore he administered an enema to himself eight times in one day, to the point that some of his intestines ulcerated and an abrasion broke out on him. He was obliged to march with ʿAlāʾ al-Dawla quickly toward Īdhaj,[110] where he was afflicted by the seizures which sometimes follow

---

* B adds:. He was asked about it and about his excesses concerning food and staying up all night and he said, "God, Who is exalted, has been generous concerning my external and internal faculties, so I use every faculty as it should be used."

القولنج. ومع ذلك فقد كان يدبّر نفسه ويحتقن للسحج ولبقيّة القولنج. فأمر يوما باتّخاذ دانقين بزر الكرفس فى جملة الحقنة طالبا لكسر ريح القولنج. فطرح بعض الأطبّاء الّذى كان يتقدّم هو إليه بمعالجته من بزر الكرفس خمسة دراهم — لست أدرى أعمدا فعله أم خطأ لأنّى لم أكن معه — فازداد السحج من حدّة البزر. وكان يتناول المثروديطوس لأجل الصرع فطرح بعض غلمانه فيه شيئا كثيرا من الأفيون وناوله إيّاه فأكله. وكان سبب

---

١) القولنج ان: علّة القولنج ب ج / / فقد ساقطة ق/ص / / ويحتقن للسحج ا ب ج ن: ويحقن نفسه لأجل السحج ق/ص

٢) فأمر ب ج ن ق/ص: وأمر ا / / بزر ا ب ج: بذر ن: من بزر ق/ص / / الحقنة ا ب ج ن: ما يحتقن به وخلطه بها ق/ص

٣) فطرح ا ب ج ن: فقصد ق/ص

٤) هو ساقطة ن / / من بزر ا ب ج: من بذر ن: وطرح من بزر ق/ص

٥) أكن ا ب ج ق/ص: أك ن / / السحج] + به ق/ص

٦) البزر ا ب ج: البذر ن: ذلك البزر ق/ص

٦—٧) فطرح . . . الأفيون ا ب ج ن: فقام بعض غلمانه وطرح شيئا كثيرا من الأفيون فيه ق/ص

٧) كثيرا ساقطة ن / / إيّاه ساقطة ق/ص

the colic. And in spite of that he treated himself and administered enemas to himself for the abrasion and for the residue of the colic. Then one day, wishing to break the wind of the colic, he ordered that two *dānaqs*[111] of celery seed be included in the enema. But one of the doctors whom he ordered to treat him threw in five *dirhams* of celery seed—I do not know | whether he did it intentionally or by mistake because I was not present—and the abrasion was aggravated by the sharpness of the seed. In addition he used to take mithridate[112] on account of the seizures, but one of his slaves threw a great quantity of opium into it; he gave it to him and he consumed it. The reason

ذلك خيانتهم فى مال كثير من خزانته فتمنّوا هلاكه ليأمنوا عاقبة أفعالهم.

ونُقِلَ الشيخ كما هو إلى إصفهان فاشتغل بتدبير نفسه. وكان من الضعف بحيث لا يستطيع القيام فلم يزل يعالج نفسه حتّى قدر على المشى. وحضر مجلس علاء الدولة وهو مع ذلك لا يتحفّظ ويكثر المجامعة ولم يبرأ من العلّة كلّ البرء وكان ينتكس ويبرأ كلّ وقت. ثمّ قصد علاء الدولة همذان وصار الشيخ معه فعاودته العلّة فى الطريق إلى أن وصل إلى همذان وعلم أنّ

---

١) خزانته ا ق/ص: خزائنه ب ج ن

٢) أفعالهم ج: أفعاله ا ب ن

٤) لا يستطيع ا ب ج ن: لا يقدر على ق/ص

٥) وهو ا ب ج ن: لكنّه ق/ص

٥–٦) لا . . . المجامعة ج ن: ساقطة ا ب: يكثر] + التخليط فى أمر ق/ص

٦) ولم ج ن ق/ص: لم ا ب / / وكان ا ب ج ن: فكان ق/ص

٧) صار ب ج: اصار ا: سار ن ق/ص / / الشيخ معه ا ب ج ن: معه الشيخ ق/ص

٨) العلّة فى الطريق ا ب ج ن: فى الطريق تلك العلّة ق/ص / / إلى همذان ا ب ن ق/ص: بهمذان ج

for this was their stealing a great deal of money from his coffers: they desired his death in order to be free from the consequences of their actions.

The Master was carried in that state to Iṣfahān, where he was occupied with taking care of himself. He was so weak that he was unable to stand, so he continued to treat himself until | he was able to walk. He attended the court of ʿAlāʾ al-Dawla, and in addition to that he did not take care and frequently had sexual intercourse. He had not completely recovered from the illness, and so he had intermittent relapses and recoveries. When ʿAlāʾ al-Dawla set out for Hamadhān, the Master went with him but the illness seized him again on the way, so that by the time he reached Hamadhān he knew that

قوّته قد سقطت وأنّها لا تفى بدفع المرض. فأهمل مداواة نفسه وكان يقول «المدبّر الّذى كان يدبّر بدنى قد عجز عن التدبير والآن فلا تنفع المعالجة.» وبقى على هذا أيّاما ثمّ انتقل إلى جوار ربّه ودفن بهمذان فى سنة ثمان وعشرين وأربعمائة. وكانت ولادته فى سنة سبعين وثلثمائة وجميع عمره ثمان وخمسون سنة. لقاه الله صالح أعماله.

---

١) قد ساقطة ن

٢) وكان ا ب ج ن: وأخذ ق/ص // يدبّر بدنى ا ج ن: يدبّرنى ب

٤) ربّه] + ورحمته ب // بهمذان] + رضى الله تعالى عنه ج // ٤٢٨ ب

٤–٦) في سنة . . . أعماله ا ب ج ن: وكان عمره ثمانيا (ثلاثا ص) وخمسين سنة وكان موته فى سنة ثمان وعشرين وأربعمائة (+ وكانت ولادته فى سنة خمس وسبعين وثلثمائة ص) ق/ص

٥) ٣٧٠ ب // وجميع ا ج ن: فجميع ب // ثمان] : ثمانى ا: ثمانية ج ن // ٥٨ ب

٦) أعماله] + وأحسن منقلبه ب: + بمنّه وكرمه ن

his strength had wasted away and that it was not sufficient to repel the illness. So he ceased treating himself and would say, "The governor who used to govern my body is now incapable of governing, and so treatment is no longer of any use." He remained like this for a few days; then he passed away into the presence of his Lord and was buried in Hamadhān in the year 428.[113] | The year of his birth was 370,[114] and so the sum of his years was 58. May God find his deeds worthy.

فهرست كتب ابن سينا

أمّا ذكره أبو عبيد الجوزجانيّ في تأريخ سيرته من فهرست كتبه فهو يقارب أربعين تصنيفا. وقد اجتهدتّ في تحصيل ما صنّف وأثبتّ في هذا الفهرست ما وجدته مضافا إلى ما ذكره الشيخ أبو عبيد ما يقارب تسعين تصنيفا:

(١) كتاب **اللواحق**. يذكر في تصانيفه أنّه شرح **الشفاء**.

(٢) كتاب **الشفاء**. يجمع جميع العلوم الأربعة. صنّف طبيعيّاته

---

١) أبو عبيد ا ج: الشيخ أبو عبيد ن

١–٤) أمّا . . . تصنيفا ا ج ن: وهذه فهرست مصنّفاته على أكمل ما وجد له ب: (وللشيخ الرئيس) من الكتب كما وجدناه غير ما هو مثبت فيما تقدّم من كلام أبي عبيد الجوز جانيّ ص

٣) صنّف ا ج: صنّفه غيره ن

٤) تصنيفا] + وتفصيله هكذا ن

٥) يذكر ا ج ن ص: ذكر ب // في تصنيفه ساقطة ب ص

٦) يجمع ا ب ن: جمع ج ص // جميع ساقطة ب // الأربعة] + فيه ص // صنّف ا ج ن: وصنّف ب ص

BIBLIOGRAPHY OF THE WORKS OF IBN SINA

As for the bibliography which Abū ʿUbayd al-Jūzjānī mentioned in his biography, it contained about forty works. However I have endeavored to collect what was written and have set down in this bibliography what I have found, added to what Shaykh Abū ʿUbayd mentioned, coming to about ninety works.[1] |

(1) The *Supplements*, mentioned in his writings as a commentary on the *Shifāʾ*. (2) The *Shifāʾ* (*Healing*), which summarizes the whole of the four sciences. He wrote the "Physics"

وإلهيّاته فى عشرين يوما بهمذان. (٣) كتاب **الحاصل والمحصول** صنّفه ببلده للفقيه أبى بكر البرقىّ فى أوّل عمره فى قريب من عشرين مجلّدة ولا يوجد إلّا نسخة الأصل. (٤) كتاب **البرّ والاثم**. صنّفه أيضا لهذا الفقيه فى الأخلاق مجلّدتان ولا يوجد إلّا عنده. (٥) كتاب **الانصاف**. عشرون مجلّدة. شرح فيه جميع كتب أرسطو وأنصف فيه بين المشرقيّين والمغربيّين. ضاع فى نهب السلطان مسعود. (٦) كتاب **المجموع**. ويعرف **بالحكمة العروضيّة**. صنّفه وله إحدى وعشرون سنة لأبى الحسن العروضىّ من غير الرياضيّات. (٧) كتاب **القانون** فى الطبّ. صنّف بعضه بجرجان

---

٣) من ساقطة ا ج // قريب من ساقطة ن

٤) لهذا الفقيه ا ب ج: للفقيه ن: للفقيه أبى بكر البرقىّ ص // مجلّدة ا ج ن ص: فى مجلّدتين ب // يوجد ا ب ن ص: يوجدان ج

٥) الإنصاف] + والاتّصاف ب // عشرون ص: عشرين ا ج ن // جميع ساقطة ن

٥–٧) عشرون . . . مسعود ساقطة ب

٦) أرسطو ا ج ن: أرسطو طاليس ص // وأنصف ا ج ص: أنصف ن

٨) إحدى وعشرون سنة ص: مآ ا: كآ سنة ب: إحدى وعشرين سنة ج ن // الحسن ا ب ج ص: الحسين ن // من غير ا ج ن ص: فيه ما سوى ب

٩) صنّف ب ج ن ص: صنّفه ا

and the "Metaphysics" in twenty days in Hamadhān. (3) The *Sum and Substance,* which he wrote in his home city for the lawyer Abū Bakr al-Baraqī in the early part of his life in about twenty volumes and which is only found in the original manuscript. (4) *Good Works and Evil,* on ethics, which he also wrote for this lawyer, in two volumes, and which is only found | in his possession. (5) The *Judgment,* in twenty volumes, in which he commented on all of the books of Aristotle and in which he judged between the Easterners and the Westerners. It was lost in Sulṭān Masʿūd's raid. (6) The *Compilation,* known as *ʿArūḍī's Philosophy,*[2] which he wrote at age twenty-one for Abū al-Ḥasan al-ʿArūḍī, leaving out the mathematics. (7) The *Qānūn* (*Canon*) of medicine, part of which he wrote in Jurjān

وبالرىّ وتمّ بهمذان وعوّل على أن يعمل له شرحا وتجارب. (٨) كتاب **الأوسط الجرجانىّ** فى المنطق. صنّفه بجرجان لأبى محمّد الشيرازىّ. (٩) كتاب **المبدأ والمعاد** فى النفس. صنفه له أيضا بجرجان. (١٠) كتاب **الأرصاد الكلّيّة** . صنّفها أيضا بجرجان لأبى محمّد الشيرازىّ. (١١) كتاب **المعاد** . صنّفه بالرىّ للملك مجد الدولة. (١٢) كتاب **لسان العرب** فى اللغة. صنّفه بإصفهان ولم ينقله إلى البياض ولا وجد له نسخة ولا مثله. (١٣) كتاب **دانش نامه العلائى** بالفارسيّة. صنّفه لعلاء الدولة بن

---

١) وبالرىّ ا ج ص: والرىّ ب: ساقطة ن / / وتمّ ا ب ج ن: وتمّه ص / / وعوّل ا ب ج ص: وعزم ن

٤) له أيضا ا ب ن ص: أيضا له ج / / بجرجان] + ووجدت فى أوّل هذا الكتاب أنّه صنّفه للشيخ أبى أحمد محمّد بن إبراهيم الفارسىّ ص / / صنّفها ا ج ن ص: صنّفه ب

٥) لأبى محمّد الشيرازىّ ا ج ن ص: له ب / / المعاد] + الأصغر ب / / بالرىّ] + وهو فى خدمة الملك مجد الدولة على هامش ب

٦) صنّفه ب ج ن ص: صنّفها ا

٧) ولا وجد ا ج ن: ولا وجدت ب: ولم يوجد ص / / مثله] + ووقع إلىّ بعض هذا الكتاب وهو غريب التصنيف ص

٨) دانش نامه العلائىّ ا ج ن : دانش مايه العلائىّ ص: دانش نامه ب. وأيضا كتاب العلائىّ بالفارسية . . . ب

and in al-Rayy, and which was finished in Hamadhān; he intended to work on a commentary and carry out experiments for it. (8) The *Middle*, or *Jurjānī*, [*Summary*] on logic, which he wrote in Jurjān for Abū Muḥammad al-Shīrāzī. (9) The *Origin and the Return*, on the soul, which he also wrote him in Jurjān.[3] (10) *Comprehensive Observations*, which he also wrote | in Jurjān for Abū Muḥammad al-Shīrāzī. (11) The *Return*, which he wrote in al-Rayy for its ruler Majd al-Dawla. (2) The *Arabic Language*, on philology, which he wrote in Iṣfahān, but did not transpose into clean copy, so nothing resembling a copy of it has been found. (13) The *ʿAlāʾī Philosphy*, in Persian, which he wrote for ʿAlāʾ al-Dawla ibn

كاكويه بإصفهان. (١٤) كتاب **النجاة**. صنفـّه فى طريق سابور خواست وهو فى خدمة علاء الدولة. (١٥) كتاب **الاشارات والتنبيهات**. وهى آخر صنـّف فى الحكمة وأجوده وكان يضنّ بها. (١٦) كتاب **الهداية** فى الحكمة. صنـّفه وهو محبوس بقلعة فردجان لأخيه علىّ يشتمل على أقسام الحكمة مختصرا. (١٧) كتاب **القولنج**. صنـّفه بهذه القلعة أيضا ولا يوجد تامـّا. (١٨) رسالة **حىّ بن يقظان**. صنـّفها بهذه القلعة أيضا رمزا عن العقل الفعـّال. (١٩) كتاب **الادوية القلبيـّة**. صنـّفها بهمذان. (٢٠) مقالة فى **النبض**

---

١) كاكويه ن ص: كالويه ا ج: خالويه ب // فى ا ج ن ص: على ب

٣) وهى ا ج ص: وهو ب ن // فى الحكمة وأجوده ساقطة ب // يضنّ ب ج ن ص: يظنّ ا

٤) بها ن ص: به ا ب ج

٥) فردجان ن ص: فرودحان ا ب ج

٦) أيضا ساقطة ب

٧) صنـّفها ا ج ن ص: صنـّفه ب // أيضا ساقطة ب

٨) صنـّفها ا ج ن ص: صنـّفه ب // بهمذان ا ب ن ص: باصفهان ج // بهمذان] + وكتب بها إلى الشريف السعيد أبى الحسين علىّ بن الحسين الحسينىّ ص: + للجبـّان على هامش ج

Kākūyah in Iṣfāhan. (14) The *Najāt*, which he wrote on the road to Sābūr Khwāst while he was in the service of ʿAlāʾ al-Dawla. (15) *Instructions and Remarks*, which is the last and best work he wrote on philosophy, to which he held steadfastly. (16) *Guidance*, on philosophy, which he wrote while a prisoner in the castle of | Fardajān for his brother ʿAlī,[4] and which contains a summary of all the branches of philosophy. (17) The *Colic*, which he wrote in that same castle and which is entirely lost. (18) The treatise *Ḥayy ibn Yaqẓān* (*Alive, the son of Awake*), also written in that castle, an allegory about the active intellect. (19) *Cardiac Drugs*, which he wrote in Hamadhān. (20) An essay on the *Pulse.*

بالفارسيّة. (٢١) مقالة فى **مخارج الحروف**. صنّفها بإصفهان للجبّان. (٢٢) رسالة إلى أبى سهل المسيحىّ فى **الزاوية**. صنفها بجرجان. (٢٣) مقالة فى **القوى الطبيعيّة** إلى أبى سعيد اليمامىّ. (٢٤) رسالة **الطير**. مرموزة يصف فيها توصّله إلى علم الحقّ. (٢٥) كتاب **الحدود**. (٢٦) مقالة فى نقض رسالة ابن الطيّب فى **القوى الطبيعيّة** . (٢٧) كتاب **عيون الحكمة**. يجمع العلوم الثلاثة. (٢٨) مقالة فى **عكوس ذوات الجهة**. (٢٩) كتاب **الموجز الكبير** فى المنطق. وأمّا **الموجز الصغير** فهو منطق **النجاة**. (٣٠) **القصيدة**

---

١) بالفارسيّة ا ج ص: فارسيّة ب ن // مخارج الحروف ا ج ن ص: أسباب حدوث الحروف ومخارجها ب // للجبّان ا ب : للجبّائىّ ن ص: ساقطة ج

٢) إلى ساقطة ا

٣) سعيد ج ن: سعد ا ب ص // اليمامىّ ا ب ن ص: اليمانىّ ج

٤) يصف فيها ا ب ج ن: تصنيف فيما ص // فيها] + عملا ب

٥) نقض ا ب ج ن: تعرض ص // ابن الطيّب ا ب ج ن: الطبيب ص

٦) يجمع ب ج ن ص: لجميع ا

٧) عكوس ا ب ج ص: علو ن

in Persian. (21) An essay on *Phonetics*, which he wrote in Iṣfahān for al-Jabbān. (22) A letter to Abū Sahl al-Masīḥī on the *Angle*, which he wrote in Jurjān.[5] (23) An essay on *Natural Faculties*[6] for Abū Saʿīd al-Yamāmī.[7] (24) The treatise, the *Bird*, an allegory in which he describes his attainment of the knowledge of the truth. (25) | *Definitions*. (26) An essay refuting the treatise of Ibn al-Ṭayyib on *Natural Faculties*.[8] (27) *Essential Philosophy*, which contains the three sciences [logic, physics, and metaphysics]. (28) An essay on the *Conversions of Modals*. (29) The *Large Epitome* on logic; as for the *Small Epitome*, it is the logic of the *Najāt*. (30) The *Ode*,

المزدوجة فى المنطق. صنّفها للسهيلىّ بكركانج. (٣١) **الخطبة التوحيديـّة** فى الإلهيـّات. (٣٢) مقالة فى **تحصيل السعادة** . وتعرف **بالحجج العشر** . (٣٣) مقالة فى **القضاء والقدر**. صنّفها فى طريق إصفهان عند خلاصة وهربه إلى إصفهان. (٣٤) مقالة فى **الهندباء**. (٣٥) مقالة فى **الاشارة الى علم المنطق** . (٣٦) مقالة فى **تقاسيم الحكمة والعلوم** . (٣٧) رسالة فى **السكنجبين**. (٣٨) مقالة فى **اللانهاية**. (٣٩) كتاب **التعاليق**. علّقه عنه ابن زيلا. (٤٠) مقالة في **خواصّ خطّ الاستواء**. (٤١) **المباحثات** بسؤال بهمنيار تلميذه

---

١) للسهيلىّ] : للسهلىّ : ا ب ج ن: للرئيس أبى الحسن سهل بن محمّد السهلىّ ص / / بكركانج ا ب ن ص : أبى بكر كانج ج / / بكركانج] + وتعرف بميزان النظر وبالأرجوزة ب / / الخطبة ا ب ج ن: الخطب ص

٢) الإلهيّات] + ظ هى الكلمة الإلهيـّة والتسبيحة ب

٣) العشر ا ب ج ن: الغر ص

٤) إلى إصفهان ا ب ج ص: إليها ن / / الهندباء] + ومنافعها ن وهامش ج

٥) تقاسيم ا ج ن ص: أقسام ب

٦) والعلوم ساقطة ب

٧) التعاليق ا ب ج ن: تعاليق ص / / عنه ابن ا ج: عند ابن ب : لابن ن: عنه تلميذه أبو منصور بن ص

٨) بهمنيار تلميذه ا ب ج ن: تلميذه أبى الحسن بهمنيار بن المرزبان ص

in couplets, on logic, which he wrote for al-Suhaylī in Gurgānj. (31) *Discourse on Unity*, in metaphysics. (32) An essay on the *Attainment of Happiness*, which is known as the *Ten Arguments*. (33) An essay on *Foreordination and Destiny*, which he wrote on the way to Iṣfahān during his escape and flight to Iṣfahān.[9] (34) An essay on *Endive*. | (35) An essay on *Instruction in the Science of Logic*. (36) An essay on the *Branches of Philosophy and the Sciences*. (37) A treatise on *Oxymel*. (38) An essay on *Infinity*. (39) *Commentaries*, which Ibn Zaylā[10] wrote at his dictation. (40) An essay on the *Characteristics of the Equator*. (41) *Discussions* about questions asked by his pupil Bahmanyār

وجوابه له. (٤٢) **عشر مسائل** أجاب عنها لأبى الريحان البيرونىّ (٤٣) جواب **ستّ عشرة مسألة** لأبى الريحان. (٤٤) مقالة فى **هيئة الارض من السماء وكونها في الوسط** . (٤٥) كتاب **الحكمة المشرقيّة** لا يوحد تامّا. (٤٦) مقالة فى **تعقّب المواضع الجدليّة**. (٤٧) مقالة فى **خطأ من قال إنّ الكمّيّة جوهريّة** . (٤٨) **المدخل الى صناعة الموسيقى**. وهو غير الموضوع فى **النجاة** . (٤٩) مقالة فى **الاجرام السماويّة**. (٥٠) مقالة فى **تدارك الخطأ الواقع في التدبير**

---

١) عشر . . . البيرونىّ ساقطة ا / / البيرونىّ ساقطة ن

٢) ستّ عشرة ص: ستّة عشر ا ب ج: ثمانية عشر ن / / الريحان ب ص: الريحان البيرونىّ ن: ريحان ا ج

٢–٥) مقالة . . . جوهريّة على هامش ب

٣) وكونها ا ج ن ص: وأنّها ب / / الوسط ب ج ن ص: السطح ا / / من السماء . . . الوسط على هامش ج

٤) لا ا ج ص: ولا ب ن

٥) مقالة ساقطة ا / / مقالة . . . جوهريّة ساقطة ص / / جوهريّة ا ن: جوهر ب ج

٦) وهو . . . النجاة على هامش ا

٧) الأجرام ا ب ن ص: الأجسام ج

and his answers to him. (42) *Ten Questions*, which he answered for Abū al-Rayḥān al-Bīrūnī.[12] (43) Answers to *Sixteen Questions* of Abū al-Rayḥān. (44) An essay on the *Position of the Earth in Relation to the Heavens and on its Existence in the Center.* (45) The *Eastern Philosophy*, which is not extant in its entirety. (46) An essay on the *Consideration of Dialectical Topics.* (47) | An essay on the *Error of Anyone Saying that Quantity Belongs to Substance.* (48) *Introduction to the Art of Music*, which is not the one found in the *Najāt.* (49) An essay on the *Celestial Bodies.* (50) An essay *Correcting the Errors in*

الطبّى.(٥١) مقالة فى **كيفيّة الرصد وتطابقه مع العلم الطبيعى**.(٥٢) مقالة فى **الأخلاق** . (٥٣) مقالة فى **آلة رصديّة** . صنّفها بإصفهان عند رصده لعلاء الدولة. (٥٤) رسالة إلى السهيلىّ فى **الكيمياء**. (٥٥) مقالة فى **غرض قاطيغورياس** . (٥٦) **الرسالة الاضحويّة في المعاد**. صنّفها للأمير أبى بكر محمّد بن عبيد. (٥٧) **معتصم الشعراء** فى العروض. صنّفه ببلاده وله سبع عشرة سنة. (٥٨) مقالة فى **حدّ الجسم**. (٥٩) **الحكمة العرشيّة**. وهو كلام مرتفع فى الالهيّات. (٦٠) **عهد** له عاهد الله به لنفسه. (٦١) مقالة فى أنّ **علم زيد غير علم عمرو**. (٦٢) كتاب **تدبير الجند**

---

١) . . . الطبّىّ (أى الرقم ٥٠) ا ب ج ن: كتاب التدارك الأنواع خطأ التدبير ص / / وتطابقه ا ب ج ن: ومطابقته ص

٣) رصده ا ج ن ص: رجوعه ورصده ب / / السهيلىّ: السهلىّ ا ب ج ن: الشيخ أبى الحسن سهل بن محمّد السهلىّ ص / / فى الكيمياء ا ج ن ص: فى أمر مستور أى الكيمياء ب

٥) صنّفها . . . عبيد ساقطة ب / / أبى بكر محمّد ا ن ص: أبى بكر بن محمّد ج

٦) صنّفه . . . سنة ساقطة ب / / سبع عشرة ن ص: سبعة عشر ا : سبع عشر ج

٨) له ساقطة ب / / لنفسه ا ب ج ص: نفسه ن

Medical Treatment. (51) An essay on the *Nature of Astronomical Observation and its Conformity with Physical Science.* (52) An essay on *Ethics.* (53) An essay on *Astronomical Instruments*, which he wrote in Iṣfahān during his observations for ʿAlāʾ al-Dawla. (54) A letter to al-Suhaylī on *Alchemy.* (55) An essay on the *Object of the "Categories"* [of Aristotle]. (56) The *Aḍḥawiyya Letter on | the Return*, which he wrote for the prince Abū Bakr Muḥammad ibn ʿUbayd.[13] (57) The *Defense of Poets*, in poetry, which he wrote in his home city when he was seventeen years old. (58) An essay on the *Definition of Body.* (59) *Throne Philosophy*, which is elevated discourse on metaphysics. (60) His *Testament*, in which he committed his soul to God. (61) An essay that the *Knowledge of Zayd is not the Knowledge of ʿAmr.* (62) The *Management and Provisioning of Soldiers*,

والمماليك والعساكر وأرزاقهم وخراج الممالك. (٦٣) مناظرات جرت له فى **النفس** مع أبى علىّ النيسابورىّ. (٦٤) خطب وتحميدات وأسجاع. (٦٥) جواب يتضمّن الاعتذار فيما نسب إليه فى هذه الخطب. (٦٦) **مختصر كتاب أوقليدس**. أظنّه المضموم إلى **النجاة.** (٦٧) مقالة فى **الأرثماطيقى.** (٦٨) عدّة قصائد وأشعار فى الزهد وغيره. يصف فيها أحواله. (٦٩) رسائل بالفارسيّة والعربيّة ومخاطبات ومكاتبات وهزليّات. (٧٠) **تعاليق على مسائل حنين** فى الطبّ. (٧١) **قوانين ومعالجات طبّيّة** . (٧٢) **عشرون مسألة** سأله عنها أهل العصر. (٧٣) **مسائل عدّة الطبّيّة.** (٧٤) مسائل

---

١) والمماليك ن ص: والممالك ا ب ج / / الممالك ا ج ن ص: الجند والممالك ب

٢) فى النفس مع . . . النيسابورىّ ا ب ج ص: مع . . . النيسابورىّ فى النفس ن / / تحميدات ا ب ج ن: تمجيدات ص

٣) فيما ا ج ن ص : عمّاب / / فى هذه ا ب ج ن : من ص

٤) كتاب ساقطة ص / / أظنّه ا ب ن ص: وأظنّه ج

٥) مقالة فى ا ب ج ن: مقالة ص / / الأرثماطيقى] + **ظ** هى الّتى فى النجاة ب / / عدّة ا ب ج ن: عشر ص

٧–٨) فى الطبّ ساقطة ب

٩) أهل ا ب ج ن: بعض أهل ص / / الطبّيّة ب ج ن ص: الطبيعيّة ا

Slave Troops, and Armies, and the Taxation of Kingdoms. (63) Disputes of his which occurred with Abū ʿAlī al-Naysābūrī[14] concerning the *Soul.* (64) Discourses, Words of Praise [to God], and Works in rhymed prose. (65) A reply containing an apology about what was attributed to him in these discourses. (66) A *Summary of Euclid,* which I think was the one added to the *Najāt.* | (67) An essay on *Arithmetic.* (68) A number of odes and poems on asceticism and other topics, in which he describes his positions. (69) Some letters, conversations, correspondence, and light works, in Arabic and Persian. (70) *Commentaries on the "Questions of Ḥunayn"*[15] concerning medicine. (71) *Medical Principles and Practice.* (72) *Twenty Questions* which his contemporaries asked him. (73) A *Number of Medical Questions.* (74) Questions

تـُدْعَى **الندور**. (٧٥) مسائل ترجمها **بالتذاكير**. (٧٦) جواب **مسائل يسيرة**. (٧٧) رسالة له إلى علماء بغداد. يسألهم الإنصاف بينه وبين رجل همذانيّ يدعى الحكمة. (٧٨) رسالة إلى صديق. يسأله الإنصاف بينه وبين هذا الهمذانيّ. (٧٩) جواب لعدّة مسائل. (٨٠) كلام له فى **تبيين مائيـّة الحزن**. (٨١) شرحه **لكتاب النفس** لأرسطو ويقال إنّه من **الانصاف**. (٨٢) مقالة فى **النفس**. تعرف **بالفصول**. (٨٣) مقالة فى **إبطال علم النجوم**. (٨٤) كتاب **الملح في النحو**. (٨٥) **فصول إلهيـّة في إثبات الاوّل**. (٨٦) فصول فى

---

١) الندور ا ب ج: النذور ن //[مسائل] . . . الندور (أى الرقم ٧٤) ساقطة ص // بالتذاكير ج ن ص: بالتذكير ا ب

٢) يسيرة ج ن: سيره ا ب: كثيرة ص // له ساقطة ب

٣) رسالة] + له ج ن

٤) هذا الهمذانىّ ا ب ج ن: الهمذانىّ الّذى يدعى الحكمة ص

٥) الحزن ب ج: الحرت ا: الحروف ن ص // شرحه لكتاب ا ب ج ن: شرح كتاب ص

٦) لأرسطو ا ب ج: لأرسطاطاليس ن: لأرسطوطاليس ص // مقالة] + له ن // تعرف ا ج ن ص: وتعرف ب

٧) مقالة] + له ن // علم ا ب ج ن: أحكام ص

٨) إلهيـّة ب ن ص: الهيئة ا ج

called *Rarities*. (75) Questions which he explained in *Notes*. (76) Answers to *Simple Questions*. (77) His letter to the *ʿulamāʾ* of Baghdād which asked them to judge between him and a man of Hamadhān who claimed to be a philosopher. (78) A letter to a friend which asks him to judge between him and this Hamadhānī. (79) Answers to a number of questions. | (80) His words *Explaining the Essence of Sorrow*. (81) His commentary on Aristotle's *De Anima*, which is said to be from the *Judgment*. (82) An essay on the *Soul*, known as the *Chapters*. (83) An essay on the *Refutaiion of the Science of Astrology*. (84) *Anecdotes on Grammar*. (85) *Metaphysical Chapters on the Proof of the First* [*Principle*]. (86) Chapters on

النفس والطبيعيّات . (٨٧) رسالة إلى أبى سعيد بن أبى الخير فى **الزهد**. (٨٨) مقالة فى أنّه **لا يجوز أن يكون شيء واحد جوهرا وعرضا**. (٨٩) مسائل جرت بينه وبين بعض الفضلاء فى فنون العلوم. (٩٠) **تعليقات** استفادها أبو الفرج الطبيب الهمذانىّ من مجلسه وجوابات له. (٩١) مقالة ذكرها فى تصانيفه أنّها فى **المسالك وبقاع الارض** . (٩٢) **مختصر في أنّ الزاوية الّتى من**

---

١) والطبيعيّات ا ب ج ن: وطبيعيّات ص // بن ساقطة ن // الخير] + رحمه الله تعالى ج: + الصوفىّ ص

٢) شيء واحد ا ب ج ص: الشيء الواحد ن

٣) بعض الفضلاء ا ج ن ص: فضلاء العصر ب

٤) أبو ا ب ن ص: ابن ج // الطبيب الهمذانىّ ا ج ن ص: الهمذانىّ الطبيب ب

٥) مقاله] + له ج // فى تصانيفه أنّها ساقطة ب

٦) المسالك ا ب ج ن: الممالك ص // وبقاع الأرض ا ب ن ص: والبقاع من الأرض ج // الّتى ساقطة ب // من ا ب ج ص: بين ن

the *Soul* and on *Physics*. (87) A letter to Abū Saʿīd ibn Abī al-Khayr[16] on *Asceticism*. (88) An essay on the *Impossibility of the Same Thing Being a Substance and an Accident*. (89) Questions which passed between him and some learned men concerning the branches of knowledge. (90) *Comments* which Abū al-Faraj, the Hamadhānī doctor,[17] posed while | in his sessions, and some answers of his. (91) An essay which is mentioned in his writings as being on the *Traveled and Uninhabited Parts of the Earth*. (92) A *Summary* [*of the position*] *that the Angle which is formed by*

المحيط والمماسّ لا كمّيّة لها ..

---

١) لها. تمّ ا وج ون فى هذا الرقم. وفى ب وص تصانيف أخرى. فى ب: **الموجز الصغير** فى المنطق. وهو منطق **عيون الحكمة**. **عيون المسائل**.

فى ص: **سبع مقالات** ألّفه لأبى الحسن أحمد بن محمّد السهلىّ. أجوبة لسؤالات سأله عنها أبو الحسن العامرى. وهى أربع عشرة مسألة. كتاب **الموجز الصغير** فى المنطق. كتاب **قيام الأرض في وسط السماء**. ألّفه لأبى الحسين أحمد بن محمّد السهلى. كتاب **مفاتيح الخزائن** فى المنطق. **كلام في الجوهر والعرض**. كتاب **تأويل الرؤيا**. مقالة فى الردّ على مقالة الشيخ أبى الفرج بن الطيّب. رسالة فى **العشق**. ألّفها لأبى عبد الله الفقيه. رسالة فى **القوى الانسانية وإدراكاتها**. قول فى **تبيين ما الحزن وأسبابه**. مقالة إلى أبى عبد الله الحسين بن سهل بن محمّد السهلىّ فى **أمر مشوب**.

*the Circumference and the Tangent has no Magnitude.**[18]

---

*Three of the MSS—A, J, and N—end on this number, but B and IAU contain other works. B adds: The *Small Epitome* on logic, which is the logic of the *Essential Philosophy;*[19] and *Main Questions.*[20]

IAU adds: *Seven Essays* which he wrote for Abū al-Ḥasan Aḥmad ibn Muḥammad al-Sahlī;[21] Answers to questions asked by Abū al-Ḥasan al-ᶜĀmirī, which are twenty-four questions;[22] the *Small Epitome* on logic; the *Position of the Earth in the Middle of the Heavens,*[23] which he wrote for Abū al-Ḥusayn Aḥmad ibn Muḥammad al-Sahlī; *Keys to the Treasures,* in logic; *Discourse on Substance and Accident;*[24] the *Interpretation of Dreams;* an essay refuting the essay of Shaykh Abū al-Faraj ibn al-Ṭayyib;[25] treatise on *Love,* which he wrote for Abū ᶜAbd Allāh, the lawyer;[26] a treatise on *Human Faculties and the Perceptions of them;* a speech *Explaining Sorrow and its Causes;*[27] an essay for Abū ᶜAbd Allāh al-Ḥusayn ibn Sahl ibn Muḥammad al-Sahlī on a *Matter of Confusion.*[28]

NOTES TO THE INTRODUCTION

1. Abū al-ᶜAbbās Aḥmad ibn al-Qāsim ibn Abī Uṣaybiᶜa wrote this work—*Essential Information about the Generations of Physicians*—*ca.* 640/1243. Muller's edition (Kônigsberg and Cairo, 1882-1884), in 2 vols., will hereinafter be cited as Ibn Abī Uṣaybiᶜa, I or II. On Ibn Abī Uṣaybiᶜa, see Carl Brockelmann, *Geschichte der arabischen Literatur*, 2nd ed., 2 vols. and 3 supplementary vols. (Leiden, 1937–1949), I, 325, and Supplement I, 560 (hereinafter referred to as *GAL*, I or II, and *GAL*, *S*, I, II, or III.)

I have used the following system of giving dates: where I have mentioned a date in the text or notes, I have given both the Muslim and Christian dates (e.g. 640/1243); when an author whom I quote gives only a Muslim date I have added the corresponding Christian date in square brackets (e.g., 754/[1353] as the date of al-Kāshī's MS.) In treating the publication data of a book I have given the date(s) as shown on the title page(s), but adding the Christian date in square brackets when only the Muslim date was given.

2. Abū al-Ḥasan ᶜAlī ibn Yūsuf al-Qifṭī, whose work—*The History of Physicians*—was written earlier than Ibn Abī Uṣaybiᶜa's. See frequent references to Ibn al-Qifṭī in Ibn Abī Uṣaybiᶜa, I, 302, 308, and II, *passim*. Lippert's edition (Leipzig, 1903) will hereinafter be referred to as al-Qifṭī. For further information on al-Qifṭī, see Lippert's introduction to the edition, pp. 5–18, and *GAL*, I, 325, and *GAL*, *S*, I, 559.

3. Ẓahīr al-Dīn Abū al-Ḥasan ᶜAlī ibn Zayd ibn Funduq al-Bayhaqī, *Supplement to the "Repository of Wisdom"*, ed. M. Shafīᶜ (Lahore, 1935), pp. 38–61. The author of this work, hereinafter referred to as Ibn Funduq, wrote this work as a continuation of the biographical *Ṣiwān al-ḥikma* of Abū Sulaymān al-Sijistānī (d. *ca.* 375/985). For further information on Ibn Funduq, see *GAL*, I, 324, and *GAL*, *S*, I, 557–58. On Abū Sulaymān, see *GAL*, I, 236, and *GAL*, *S*, I, 377.

4. Aḥmad ibn Muḥammad ibn Khallikān, *Wafayāt al-aᶜyān* (*The Obituaries of Notables*), trans. W. de Slane, 4 vols. (Paris, 1842–1871).

5. Ibid., I, 440–44.

6. ᶜAbd al-Ḥayy ibn al-ᶜImād, *Shadharāt al-dhahab fī akhbār man dhahab* (*Nuggets of Gold in the Affairs of Those Who have Departed*), 8 vols. (Beirut, 1965), III, 234-237. For Ibn al-ᶜImād, see *GAL*, *S*, II, 403.

7. A. F. al-Ahwānī, ed., *Nukat fī aḥwāl al-Shaykh al-Raʾīs Ibn Sīnā* (*Stories Concerning the Experiences of the Shaykh al-Raʾīs Ibn Sīnā*), by Yaḥyā ibn Aḥmad al-Kāshī, in *Dhikrā Ibn Sīnā* (*Avicenna Memorial*), No. 3 (Cairo, 1952), pp. 6–7.

8. For further information on al-Kāshī, see *GAL*, *S*, II, 280, where the date of his death is given as 707/1307–08. The colophon of the manuscript, however, states that it was finished in 754/[1353].

For further information on Muḥammad ibn Maḥmūd Shahrazūrī (*fl.* 7th/13th century), see *GAL*, I, 468, and *GAL*, *S*, I, 850.

9. Al-Ahwānī, Introduction, p. 7.

10. Ibid.

11. *Sar-gudhasht-i Ibn-i Sīnā* (*Biography of Ibn Sīnā*) (Teheran, 1331/[1952]).

12. Ibid., Introduction (not paginated).

13. This date is agreed upon by the two major recent bibliographies: Yahya Mahdavi, *Fihrist-i muṣannafāt-i Ibn-i Sīnā* (*Bibliography of the Works of Ibn Sīnā*), Publications of the University of Teheran, No. 206 (Teheran, 1333/1954), p. 335, n. 3. Also Father G. C. Anawati, *Muʾallafāt Ibn Sīnā* (*The Works of Ibn Sīnā*) (Cairo, 1950), p. 114.

14. Mahdavi, *passim*, pp. 331–371.

15. Mahdavi, p. 338, n. 1. Anawati, p. 13, dates it from the 9th/15th century.

16. Mahdavi, p. 330, n. 2. Anawati, p. 262, gives the 10th/16th century.

17. Mahdavi, p. 337, n. 1, and Anawati, p. 136.

18. In this recension, as in the rest of the presentation of this critical edition, I follow the procedure set down in Paul Maas, *Textual Criticism*, trans. from the 3rd German edition by Barbara Flower (Oxford, 1958), pp. 2–24, See especially p. 4, which gives the reasons for discarding certain witnesses.

19. Mahdavi, p. 371, n. 2. Anawati does not describe this manuscript.

20. Mahdavi, p. 333, n. 2. Anawati, p. 264, gives the date 1242/[1827].

21. Anawati, p. 290. Mahdavi does not describe this manuscript.

22. Mahdavi, p. 337, n. 3. This manuscript is located in Aya Sofya, MS. 4849(1), is written in large, clear *naskhī* script, 12x22 cm., 21 lines/page, and is dated 697/[1298]. Anawati, p. 117, dates it 657/[1259].

23. In preparing this stemma, I have followed Paul Maas's discussion of "stemmatics," including his definition of separative and conjunctive errors, etc., found on pp. 42–49 of *Textual Criticism.*

24. *Avicenna on Theology*, in The Wisdom of the East Series (London, 1951), pp. 9–24.

25. On p. 20, Arberry lists the three letter writers as Ibn al-ʿAmīd, al-Ṣāḥib, and al-Ṣābī, in that order, which is the order found in al-Qifṭī, but not in Ibn Abī Uṣaybiʿa, who reverses the order of al-Ṣāḥib and al-Ṣābī. See below, "Notes to the Translation of the Autobiography/Biography," nn. 95, 96, 97.

26. For further information on these translations, see "Notes to the Translation of the Autobiography/Biography."

27. See al-Qifṭī, pp. 417, line 18, and 421, line 3, for the poetry, and p. 423, lines 17-23, for the anecdotes.

28. See, *inter alia*, G. M. Wickens, ed., *Avicenna: Scientist and Philosopher* (London, 1952), pp. 9–28, for Arberry's translation plus his own running commentary and a translation of Ibn Sina's poem on the soul; also see Arberry, *Aspects of Islamic Civilization* (Ann Arbor, 1967), pp. 136–46, with no changes in the translation; and C. M. Brand, ed., *Icon and Minaret* (Englewood Cliffs, N. J., 1969), pp. 156–59, for Arberry's translation of the autobiography only.

29. S. M. Afnan, *Avicenna: His Life and Works* (London, 1958), ch. ii, "Life and works of Avicenna," pp. 57–82. For further information on Niẓāmī ʿArūḍī and the *Chahār maqāla*, see below, "Notes to the Translation of the Autobiography/Biography," nn. 41 and 43.

30. S. H. Nasr, *Three Muslim Sages* (Cambridge, Mass., 1964), pp. 20–24. See also Nasr's *Introduction to Islamic Cosmological Doctrines* (Cambridge, Mass., 1964), ch. xi, "The Life and works of Ibn Sīnā and his significance," pp. 177-81, for similar material.

31. P. K. Hitti, *Makers of Arab History* (New York, 1968), "Ibn Sīnā: prince of physicians and philosophers," pp. 202–18.

32. Anawati, *Muʾallafāt.*

33. Mahdavi, pp. 307–24.

34. For this number, see below, "Bibliography of the Works of Ibn Sīnā."

35. See, e.g., p. 81, where *ʿUyūn al-masāʾil,* No. 16 in his bibliography, is stated to be the work of al-Fārābī.

36. Ibn Funduq, pp. 46–47.

37. Ibid., pp. 187–190.

38. See Appendix I for these omissions and additions.

39. See Appendix II for these omissions.

40. See above, p. 4.

41. See above, pp. 3-4.

42. See above, pp. 46–49.

NOTES TO THE TRANSLATION OF THE AUTOBIOGRAPHY / BIOGRAPHY

1. "Balkh": one of the four capitals of Khurāsān. See Yāqūt, *Muʿjam al-buldān*, ed. F. Wüstenfeld, 6 vols. (Leipzig, 1866–73), I, 713–14. See also the description of the city in G. Le Strange, *The Lands of the Eastern Caliphate* (Cambridge, 1905; rpt. New York, 1966), pp. 420–23. Also see R. N. Frye, "Balkh," *Encyclopaedia of Islam*, 2nd ed. (Leiden and London, 1960–), I, 1000–02. (Hereinafter to be referred to as *EI*².)

2. "Bukhārā": one of the chief cities of Transoxiana and capital of the Sāmānid dynasty (204/819–395/1005). See Yāqūt, *Buldān*, I, 517–22, Le Strange, pp. 460–63, and W. Barthold-R. N. Frye, "Bukhārā," *EI*², I, 1293–96.

3. "Nūḥ ibn Manṣūr": al-Amīr al-Riḍā Abū al-Qāsim Nūḥ II (r. 365/976–387/997). See Ibn al-Athīr, *al-Kāmil fī al-tārīkh*, ed. C. J. Tornberg (Leiden, 1851–76; rpt. Beirut, 1966), IX, 129, *s.a.* 387, where his death is said to have occurred in the month of Rajab. But Gardīzī, *Zayn al-Akhbār*, ed. ʿAbd al-Ḥayy Ḥabībī (Teheran, 1347 [1969]), p. 164, says that he died in Shaʿbān of that year.

4. "royal estates": estates which paid the tithe (*ʿushr*) rather than the land tax (*kharāj*). During this period the largest owner of these estates was the Caliph, followed by the various princes and governors. See C. Cahen, "Dayʿa," *EI*², II, 187–88.

5. "Kharmaythan": one of the villages in the territory of Bukhārā. Yāqūt, *Buldān*, II, 426, gives the voweling as above. But al-Samʿānī, *Kitāb al-ansāb*, ed. D. S. Margoliouth in facsimile, Gibb Memorial Series, XX (London, 1912), fol. 195b, gives the voweling as Khurmīthan.

6. "Afshana": one of the villages in the territory of Bukhārā. See Yāqūt, *Buldan*, I, 330.

7. "my mother": her name is given as Sitārah by Ibn Funduq, p. 39, as well as by J.

8. "in Ṣafar, 370 ... Sirius": Ibn Funduq, p. 39, gives the same date of birth and includes the same astrological information as the margin of J. For further information on this horoscope, see al-Bīrūnī, *Kitāb al-tafhīm li-awāʾil ṣināʿat al-tanjīm* (*The Book of Instruction in the Elements of the Art of Astrology*), ed. and trans. R. Ramsay Wright (London, 1934), p. 258, where the degree of exaltation is explained: "There are certain signs which are described as places of exaltation (*sharaf*) of the planets, like the thrones of kings and other high positions." He then gives the degrees of exaltation of the planets: Jupiter, 15 degrees of Cancer; the Moon, 3 degrees of Taurus; the Sun, 19 degrees of Aries; Venus, 27 degrees of Pisces. Later, on p. 279, he defines the Lot of Fortune: "The Lot of Fortune is a point of the Zodiac,

the distance of which from the degree of the ascendant in the direction of the succession of signs is equal to the distance of the moon from the sun in the opposite direction." On p. 283, al-Bīrūnī defines the Lot of the Unseen: "The reciprocal of the Lot of Fortune is the Lot of the Sun, which is the Lot of the Unseen and Religion (*sahm al-ghayb wa'l-dīn*)."

9. "my brother": His brother is called Maḥmūd by Ibn Funduq, p. 39, as well, and he adds that Maḥmūd was born five years after Ibn Sīnā. However, in the bibliographies found in the manuscripts, a treatise is described as being written for his brother ᶜAlī. See above, pp. 96–97.

10. "literature": *adab*. The meaning of this term changed several times from the pre-Islamic period to the time of Ibn Sīnā. It could mean either the quality of urbanity, courtesy, and elegance of a Jāḥiẓ (d. 255/868) or Ibn Sīnā's older contemporary Abū Ḥayyān al-Tawḥīdī (d. ca. 414/1023), or it could mean the humanistic literature which encompassed elements of Arab, Iranian, Indian, and Greek cultures. But during the lifetime of Ibn Sīnā, the concept of *adab* was becoming narrowed to mean the knowledge necessary for a particular position or function. Ibn Sīnā here seems to mean the broader definition of the term. See F. Gabrieli, "Adab," *EI*², I, 175–76.

11. "the Ismāᶜīliyya": In Khurāsān and Transoxiana at this time the propaganda for the Fāṭimid cause was called *daᶜwat-i Miṣriyyān*. See M. Canard, "Daᶜwa," *EI*², II, 169; see also S. M. Stern, "The Early Ismāᶜīlī Missionaries in North-West Persia and in Khurāsān and Transoxania," *Bulletin of the School of Oriental and African Studies*, XXIII (1960), pp. 56–90.

Ismāᶜīlī propaganda won a large number of adherents earlier in the reign of the Sāmānids, but the heresy was suppressed ca. 330/942 by the Amīr al-Saᶜīd Naṣr II (r. 301/914–331/943) and his son, the Amīr al-Ḥamīd Nūḥ I (r. 331/943–343/954). See Niẓām al-Mulk, *Siyar al-mulūk* (or *Siyāsat nāmah*), ed. H. Darke (Teheran, 1340/1962), pp. 267–75; also trans. H. Darke, *The Book of Government or Rules for Kings* (London, 1960), pp. 218–24. Also see W. Barthold, *Turkestan Down to the Mongol Invasion*, 3rd ed., Gibb Memorial Series, V (London, 1968), pp. 242–44. Niẓām al-Mulk also states that the Bāṭinīs or Qarmaṭīs, as he calls them, emerged in the fifteenth year of the reign of the Amīr al-Sadīd Manṣūr I (r. 350/961–365/976) and were decisively put down, so that "this sect completely collapsed, to the point that none of them were even remembered." Niẓām al-Mulk, pp. 278–84, trans., pp. 227–33. However, Barthold, reflecting the views of the historians of that time, states, "The remainder of Manṣūr's reign [i.e., after the struggle for the Amīrate following his brother's death in 350/961, which lasted for about a year], so far as is known, passed off peacefully." *Turkestan*, p. 251.

12. "philosophy": *falsafa*. Greek philosophy, with gnostic and Neoplatonic overtones. See R. Arnaldez, "Falsafa," *EI*², II, 769–75.

"geometry": *al-handasa*. "An Arabized Persian term, this craft was called geometry in Greek ..." al-Khwārazmī, *Kitāb mafātīḥ al-ᶜulūm*, ed. G. van Vloten (Leiden, 1895; rpt. Leiden, 1968), p. 202.

"Indian calculation": *ḥisāb al-hind*. This form of calculation, using the "Indian" numerals, was being superseded by *ḥisāb al-ᶜaqd*, or dactylonomy, during the 4th/

10th–5th/11th centuries. In fact, Ḥamd Allāh Mustawfī says that Ibn Sīnā invented a method of calculation by dactylonomy in 420/1029, thus freeing accountants from the bother of using counters. C. Pellat, "Ḥisāb al-ᶜAḳd, " *EI*², III, 466.

"Rasā'il Ikhwān al-Ṣafā'": Both J and Ibn Funduq, p. 40, add that he and his father studied the *Treatises* (*Treatise,* in Ibn Funduq) *of the Sincere Bretheren.*

13. "Indian calculation ... (the Mathematician)": Ibn Funduq, p. 40, also adds that Ibn Sīnā studied geometry and algebra with this man, whom he also calls Maḥmūd al-Massāḥī.

14. "al-Nātilī": He is called al-Ḥakīm Abū ᶜAbd Allāh Ḥusayn ibn Ibrāhīm al-Ṭabarī al-Nātilī by Ibn Funduq, p. 22. His *nisba,* al-Nātilī, is taken from the villlage of Nātil (or Nātila) in Ṭabaristān. See Yāqūt, *Buldān,* IV, 726, where he lists two other scholars from that place, but neither he nor al-Samᶜāni lists AbūᶜAbd Allāh. Ibn Abī Uṣaybiᶜa, I, 240, lists him as a physician.

15. "jurisprudence": *fiqh.* The branch of study dealing with the religious law (*sharīᶜa*) of Islam. See I. Goldziher-J. Schacht, "Fiḳh," *EI*², II, 886–91.

16. "Ismāᶜil the Ascetic": *al-zāhid.* He is not listed in the standard biographical dictionaries.

17. *"Isagoge": īsāghūjī.* Porphyry's introduction to the *Organon* of Aristotle, it "was used for many centuries in the east and west as the clearest and most practical manual of Aristotelian logic ...." De Lacy O'Leary, *How Greek Science Passed to the Arabs* (London, 1949), pp. 26–27. Both al-Khwārazmī and Ibn al-Nadīm use this term as transliterated from the Greek and translate it as the introduction (*madkhal*) to other works on logic. al-Khwārazmī, *Mafātīḥ,* p. 141; Ibn al-Nadīm, *al-Fihrist,* ed. G. Flugel, 2 vols. (Leipzig, 1871–72; rpt. Beirut, 1964), I, 253.

18. "genus": *jins.* The first of the five predicables, used by the Muslim logicians more precisely than by the original Greek users of the word. See A. M. Goichon, *Lexique de la langue Philosophique d'Ibn Sīnā* (Paris, 1938), pp. 48–49; also see S. van den Bergh, "Djins," *EI*², II, 550.

19. "that which is predicated": *maqūl.* See Goichon, *Lexique,* p. 320.

20. "Euclid": the *Elements,* called the *Elements of Geometry* (*uṣūl al-handasa*) by Ibn al-Nadīm, *Fihrist,* I, 265. He also transliterates the Greek as *al-astrūshiya.* al-Qifṭī, p. 62, gives the same two titles. Ibn Khaldūn, *al-Muqaddima* (*Cairo,* n.d.), p. 486, says that it is called the *Elements* (*uṣūl*) or *First Principles* (*arkān*). This passage is translated by F. Rosenthal, *The Muqaddimah,* Bollingen Series XIIII, 3 vols. (New York, 1958), III, 130.

21. "the *Almagest": al-majisṭī.* Claudius Ptolemy's *Syntaxis Mathematica.* See al-Qifṭī, pp. 95–98, and Ibn al-Nadīm, *Fihrist,* pp. 267–68.

22. "Gurgānj": the capital of the province of Khwārazm. See Yāqūt, *Buldān,* IV, 260–61. Ibn Funduq, p. 40, also says that al-Nātilī went to the court of Abū ᶜAlī M'amūn ibn Muhammad, the Khwārazm-shāh. Since he did not become Khwārazm-shāh until 385/995, Ibn Sīnā, according to this account, must have been

at least 15 years old when al-Nātilī left. See C.E. Bosworth, *The Islamic Dynasties*, Islamic Surveys, No. 5 (Edinburgh, 1967), p. 107.

23. "metaphysics": *al-ilāhiyyāt*, divine matters. *ʿIlm ilāhī* is one of the terms for metaphysics, also called *mā baʿda al-ṭabīʿa* (that which is after physics). Goichon, *Lexique*, p. 241.

24. "set of files": *ẓuhūr*. Ibn Funduq, p. 40, says *ẓuhūr min al-qarāṭīs* (a file of scrolls).

25. "classification": See Goichon, *Lexique*, p. 340, where she attempts to classify the types of syllogism, noting that Ibn Sīnā did not specifically do so.

26. "drink a cup of wine . . .": This statement, as well as other references to his more hedonistic pursuits, gave ammunition to many later critics. In fact, Ibn Funduq adds at this point, p. 41, "the principal philosophers like Plato and others were ascetics, but Abū ʿAlī differed from their path and habit and loved to drink wine and exhaust his sexual strength; then everyone who followed him imitated him in immorality and abandonment."

27. "logical, natural, and mathematical sciences": But Ibn Funduq, p. 42, states that he was poor in mathematics, because "a person who has tasted the sweetness of metaphysics is niggardly in spending his thoughts in mathematics, so he fancies it from time to time and then abandons it."

28. "*Metaphysics*": *kitāb mā baʿda al-ṭabīʿa*. Ibn al-Nadīm, *Fihrist*, I, 251, calls it *kitab al-ḥurūf* (*The Letters*), also known as *al-ilāhiyyāt*, with sections arranged on the basis of the Greek alphabet. It was translated, wholly or in part, by Isḥāq ibn Ḥunayn (d. 298/910), Abū Zakariyyā Yaḥyā ibn ʿAdī (d. 364/975), and Asṭāth, whose translation for al-Kindī (d. after 257/870) was used by Ibn Rushd (Averroës, d. 595/1198). See R. Walzer, *Greek into Arabic*, Oriental Studies, No. 1 (Oxford, 1962), p. 90.

29. "salesman": He is called Muḥammad al-Dallāl (the Salesman) by Ibn Funduq, p. 42.

30. "Abū Naṣr al-Fārābī": Muḥammad ibn Muḥammad ibn Ṭarkhān (d. 339/950). He was known as the "second teacher," the first being Aristotle. See R. Walzer, "al-Fārābī," *EI*², II, 778–81.

"on . . . *Metaphysics*": There are two extant works by al-Fārābī which could be the book Ibn Sīnā bought. The first of these, "On the Objects of the Philosopher (*al-ḥakīm*) in Each Section of the Book Marked by Letters, Being a Determination of the Object of Aristotle in the *Metaphysics*," was edited by Friedrich Dieterici, *Alfārābī's Philosophische Abhandlungen* (Leiden, 1890), pp. 34–38. However, this work is little more than a table of contents of the *Metaphysics* and would hardly be the book which so profoundly impressed Ibn Sīnā. There is more likelihood of its being the recently discovered *Kitab al-ḥurūf*, ed. by Muhsin Mahdi as *Alfarabi's Book of Letters* (Beyrouth, 1969). This is a much longer work—over 160 pages in the edition—in which al-Fārābī analyzes the *Metaphysics* in some detail.

31. "Sulṭān": Perhaps Ibn Sīnā is using the term in its abstract sense, with the

meaning of sovereign power, rather than the meaning which it later came to have: governor or ruler. I know of no other instance of the Sāmānids' being referred to as "Sulṭān." See E. W. Lane, *Arabic-English Lexicon* (London, 1863–93; rpt. New York, 1956), Bk. I, pt. 4, pp. 1405—06.

32. "in his service": Ibn Funduq, p. 43, adds, "physicians [or philosophers: *ḥukamāʾ*] before that time used to be proud and did not approach the doors of rulers."

In the margin of J the statement is found that Nūḥ ibn Manṣūr was cured by Ibn Sīnā. However, the Sāmānid ruler cannot have lived very long after his meeting Ibn Sīnā, since the date of his death is given as Rajab or Shaʿbān, 387/997 (see above, n. 3.) If Ibn Sīnā was about seventeen and one-half years old when he was called to the court, as his account would seem to indicate, the date must have been very near Rajab, 387.

33. "the ancients": *al-awāʾil*, probably meaning the Greeks.

34. "I read these books ... science": Ibn Funduq, p. 43, adds, "a fire broke out in this library and the books were totally destroyed. Some of the opponents of Abū ʿAlī said that he set fire to those books in order to appropriate these sciences and precious [knowledge] for himself and cut off the sources of these useful [sciences] from their adherents; but God knows best."

35. "Abū al-Ḥasan, the Prosodist": *al-ʿArūḍī*. He is called Abū al-Ḥasan Aḥmad ibn ʿAbd Allāh in the text of the surviving work which purports to be the one Ibn Sīnā wrote for him. See *Kitāb al-majmūʿ*, ed. Dr. S. Sālim (Cairo, 1969), p. 33. This *kunya* (Abū al-Ḥasan) is not mentioned by al-Samʿānī, *Ansāb*, fol. 389a.

36. "Abū Bakr al-Baraqī": al-Samʿānī, fol. 75a, says that Baraqī is the correct voweling, since the name comes from the Persian *barah*, which means crown prince. It was a great family in Khwārazm, descended from the Khwārazm-shāhs, which had moved to Bukhārā. al-Samʿānī's information about Abū Bakr came from Abū Bakr's son Abū ʿAbd Allāh through Abū al-Ḥasan (or Abū Naṣr, see below) ibn Mākūlā (d. 485/1092), who stated, "Abū Bakr Aḥmad ibn Muḥammad was one of the foremost exponents of literature, Ṣūfism, theology [*kalām*], ... and poetry. ... I have seen a *diwān* of his poetry, most of which was in the handwriting of his pupil, Ibn Sīnā, the philosopher." However, Ibn Mākūlā adds that Abū Bakr died in Muḥarram, 376, when Ibn Sīnā was only six years old and had just moved to Bukhārā. One of Abū Bakr's sons, Abū ʿAbd Allāh Muḥammad, studied with his father and may have dictated the poetry to Ibn Sīnā. According to Ibn Mākūlā, Abū ʿAbd Allāh was famous for his ability in jurisprudence, poetry, and philology. He worked in the administration of Bukhārā, first under the Sāmānids, then under "Ṭamghāj-khān," who overthrew the Sāmānids in 389/999. Perhaps Ibn Sīnā means Abū ʿAbd Allāh ibn Abū Bakr in this passage. See al-Samʿānī, *Ansāb*, fol. 75a. For Ibn Mākūlā, see *GAL*, I, 354, and *GAL, S*, I, 602; see also Yāqūt, *Irshād al-arīb*, ed. D. S. Margoliouth, Gibb Memorial Series, VI (Leiden and London, 1907–27), V, 435-where he is called Abū Naṣr ʿAlī ibn Hibat Allāh ibn Mākūlā.

37. "*The Sum and Substance* ... volumes": Ibn Funduq, p. 44, adds, "and a copy of it in the library of Būzajān was lost."

38. *"Good Works and Evil"*: Ibn Funduq, p. 44, adds, "I saw a copy of it in the possession of the Imām Muḥammad al-Ḥārithān al-Sarakhsī (may God have mercy on him), in a crabbed hand, in the year 544/[1149]."

39 "my father died": According to Ibn Funduq, p. 44, Ibn Sīnā's father died when he was 22 years old; i.e., in 392/1002.

40. "Necessity led me to ... Gurgānj": As Ibn Funduq, pp. 44–45, puts it: "When the affairs of the Sāmānids became disordered, necessity led him to leave Bukhārā and move to Gurgānj."

A problem of dating this move to Gurgānj arises when one considers that the last Sāmānid to rule in Bukhārā, Abū al-Fawāris ᶜAbd al-Malik ibn Nūḥ was deposed and imprisoned by the Qarākhānid Ilig Naṣr ibn ᶜAlī in 389/999 (Gardīzī, *Zayn*, p. 173; Barthold, *Turkestan*, p. 268). However, another of Nuḥ's sons, Abū Ibrāhīm Ismāᶜil, escaped and made numerous attempts to return to power in Bukhārā; he was finally defeated and killed in 395/1005 (Gardīzī, pp. 175–76; Barthold, pp. 269–70). Ibn Sīnā must have moved from Bukhārā to Gurgānj between 392/1002 and 395/1005, and the "administrative post of the Sultān" most probably was in the regime of the Ilig Naṣr.

41. "Abū al-Ḥusayn al-Suhaylī": In all of the sources of this edition, as well as in Ibn Funduq, p. 45, he is called al-Sahlī. However, Abū Manṣūr ᶜAbd al-Malik ... al-Thaᶜālibī, *Yatīmat al-dahr*, ed. Muḥammad Muḥyī al-Dīn ᶜAbd al-Ḥamīd, 2nd ed. (Cairo, 1375/1956), IV, 254, gives his name as Abū al-Ḥusayn Aḥmad ibn Muḥammad al-Suhaylī, as does Yāqūt, *Irshād*, II, 202, who says he went to Baghdād in 404/[1013–14] and died there in 418/[1027]. This *nisba* (al-Suhaylī) is also given by Muḥammad Qazwīnī in his notes to the *Chahār maqāla* of Niẓāmī ᶜArūḍī, although the text of the work reads "al-Sahli". See Niẓāmī ᶜArūḍī, *Chahār maqāla*, ed. Muhammad Qazwīnī, Gibb Memorial Series, XI, No. 1 (Leiden and London, 1910), p. 76 (text), and p. 244 (notes).

42. "ᶜAlī ibn Maʾmūn": Abū al-Ḥasan ᶜAlī ibn Maʾmūn ibn Muḥammad, Khwārazm-shāh (r. 387/997–399/1009), a patron of scholars.

43. "necessity led me": According to the story told by Niẓāmī ᶜArūḍī, Ibn Sīnā was forced to leave Gurgānj when Maḥmūd of Ghazna (r. 388/998–421/1030) demanded that the Khwārazm-shāh Abū al-ᶜAbbās Maʾmūn ibn Maʾmūn (r. 399/1009–407/1017) send a number of learned men, including Ibn Sīnā, from Gurgānj to Ghazna. The Khwārazm-shāh informed these men of Maḥmūd's demand, and some of them went willingly, or resignedly, to Maḥmūd's court, but Ibn Sīnā and another scholar, Abū Sahl al-Masīḥī, chose to flee to the court of Qābūs (see below, n. 50). After a harrowing journey across the desert south of Gurgānj, during which time Abū Sahl died, Ibn Sīnā finally reached Jurjān and the safety of Qābūs's patronage. See E. G. Browne, A *Literary History of Persia* (Cambridge, 1902–24; rpt. Cambridge, 1956), II, 95–97.

This account, however, cannot be accurate as it stands for several reasons. The scholars were taken to Ghazna by Maḥmūd at the time of his conquest of Khwārazm in 407/1017, as we know from the case of al-Bīrūnī (d. after 442/1050), one of those who chose to go to Ghazna in Niẓāmī ᶜArūḍī's story. See Ibn al-Athīr, IX, 264–65, *s.a.* 407; and D. G. Boilot, "al-Bīrūnī," *EI*², I, 1236. Since Qābūs was deposed in

402/1012 and killed in 403/1013 (see below, n. 50), Ibn Sīnā must have left Gurgānj before 402/1012. Boilot suggests the date 398/1008, but since Ibn Sīnā's companion, Abū Sahl al-Masīḥī, wrote at least one work dedicated to the Khwārazm-shāh Abū al-ᶜAbbās Maʾmūn ibn Maʾmūn, the date of departure must have been some time after 399/1009, the date of his accession. See Ibn Abī Uṣaybiᶜa, I, 328, for Abū Sahl's life and works. In addition, Ibn Sīnā was in Hamadhān , at the court of Shams al-Dawla, by 405/1015 (see below, nn. 63, 66).

44. "Nasā": A city in Khurāsān south of Gurgānj, part of the domains of the Khwārazm-shāh. See Yāqūt, *Buldān*, IV, 776; Le Strange, p. 394. It is also voweled Nisā.

45. "Bāward": A city one day's journey from Nasā, also under the suzerainty of the Khwārazm-shāhs. It is also spelled Abīward. See Yāqūt, *Buldān*, I, 111; Le Strange, p. 394.

46. "Ṭūs": The second city of the Naysābūr (Nīshāpūr) quarter of Khurāsān. After 389/999 it was under the control of Maḥmūd of Ghazna. See Yāqūt, *Buldān*, III, 560-62; Le Strange, p. 388; Barthold, *Turkestan*, p. 266.

47. "Samanqān": A territory near Jājarm (see next note), one of the districts of Naysābūr. It is also spelled Samalqān. See Yāqūt, *Buldān*, III, 145; Le Strange, p. 392.

al-Qifṭī and Ibn Abī Uṣaybiᶜa add Shaqqān to this itinerary, but he probably did not enter this village, called "one of the villages of Naysābūr" by Yāqūt, *Buldān*, III, 306. Ibn Funduq, p. 46, in giving the same itinerary as the other sources of this edition, mentions parenthetically, "but he did not enter Naysābūr."

48. "Jājarm": A town which is the main center of a large district situated between Naysābūr and Jurjān. See Yāqūt, *Buldān*, II, 4; Le Strange, pp. 392, 430.

49. "Jurjān": The name of both a province on the southeast shore of the Caspian Sea and its capital city. At this time the province was ruled by the Ziyārids as clients of the Ghaznavids. See Yāqūt, *Buldān*, II, 48–54; Le Strange, pp. 376–78; Bosworth, *Dynasties*, pp. 92–93.

50. "Amīr Qābūs": Shams al-Maᶜālī Qābūs ibn Wushmagīr (r. 367/978–402/1012), a poet and patron of poets and scholars, he took part in the dynastic struggles between the Būyids and the Sāmānids for control of Khurāsān and Jurjān, usually on the side of the Sāmānids, where he spent a great deal of time in exile. After the fall of the Sāmānids he was forced to accept the suzerainty of the Ghaznavids. See al-Thaᶜālibī, *Yatīma*, IV, 59–61; Yāqūt, *Irshād*, VI, 143–52; Bosworth, *Dynasties*, p. 92.

51. "the seizure of Qābūs . . . his death there": His deposition and imprisonment took place in 402/1012 and his death came in 403/1013. Ibn al-Athīr, IX, 238–40, *s.a.* 403.

52. "Dihistān": The name of a district, and its capital city, north of Jurjān, toward Khwārazm. See Yāqūt, *Buldān*, II, 633; Le Strange, p. 379.

53. "Abū ᶜUbayd al-Jūzjānī": His full name was Abū ᶜUbayd ᶜAbd al-Wāḥid

ibn Muḥammad al-Jūzjānī. The pupil and biographer of Ibn Sīnā, he added the sections on mathematics to the *Najāt* and the *ᶜAlāʾī*, and wrote commentaries on the *Qānūn* and *Ḥayy ibn Yaqẓān*. Ibn Funduq quotes one of his teachers as saying, "In the coterie of Abū ᶜAli, Abū ᶜUbayd seemed like a novice (*murīd*) rather than a learned pupil (*mustafīd*)." Ibn Funduq, pp. 93–94. He is not mentioned in al-Samᶜānī or Yāqūt, *Īrshād*.

Jūzjān, the place from which Abū ᶜUbayd received his *nisba*, is written also al-Jūzjānān or Jūzajān, and is a district to the west of Balkh in Khurāsān. See Yāqūt, *Buldān*, II, 149-50; Le Strange, p. 423.

54. "Abū Muḥammad al-Shīrāzī: He is not mentioned in the standard biographical dictionaries. For further information on this person, see below, "Notes to the Translation of the Bibliography," n. 3.

55. "mountain country": *arḍ al-jabal*. Usually this area is called the province of Jibāl, or *al-ᶜirāq al-ᶜajamī* (Persian ᶜIraq), but it is called *bilād al-jabal* by Abū al-Fiḍā (cited by Le Strange, p. 185) and *balad al-jabal* by Ibn al-Athīr, IX, *passim*.

56. "a catalogue of all of his books": This list is found only in al-Qifṭī and Ibn Abī Uṣaybiᶜa, although a similar list is found in Ibn Funduq, pp. 46–47. See the "Introduction to the Bibliographies" and Appendix I of this work.

57. "*Modals*": *dhawāt al-jiha*. See Goichon, *Lexique*, p. 427.

58. "al-Rayy": Largest of the four capital cities of the Jibāl in the 4th/10th century, according to Yāqūt, *Buldān*, II, 890–921, following Iṣṭakhrī (first half of the 4th/10th century) and Ibn Ḥawqal (who travelled between 331/943 and 357/968). The other three capitals were Qirmīsīn, Hamadhān, and Iṣfahān. See Le Strange, pp. 186, 214; Ibn Ḥawqal, *Sūrat al-ard*, ed. M. J. de Goeje, *Bibliotheca Geographorum Arabicorum*, II (Leiden, 1873), p. 363; S. Maqbūl Aḥmad, "Djughrāfiyā," *EI*², II, 582.

59. "al-Sayyida": The widow of Fakhr al-Dawla ᶜAlī (d. 387/997), the previous Būyid ruler of al-Rayy. Her name is given as Shirīn by Yāqūt, *Buldān*, III, 211, and by Paul Casanova, "Les Ispehbeds de Firim," in *A Volume of Oriental Studies Presented to Professor Edward G. Browne* (Cambridge, 1922), p. 122, who says that her father was the Ispahbad, or governor, of Firim.

She assumed the regency for her young son, Majd al-Dawla (see next note), upon the death of his father, but refused to relinquish it when he attained his majority. She instead kept him distracted by encouraging his pursuit of the pleasures of drinking and the harem. See Ibn al-Athīr, IX, 131—32, 369, *s.a.* 387 and 419.

60. "Majd al-Dawla": Abū Ṭālib Rustam ibn Fakhr al-Dawla ᶜAlī, he was four years old when his father died and his mother assumed control of the state. He reigned until the death of his mother in 419/1028, at which point the troops rebelled and he called in Maḥmūd of Ghazna to help put down the revolts. This Maḥmūd did, incidentally deposing Majd al-Dawla and taking him back to Ghazna as a prisoner. See Ibn al-Athīr, IX, 371—72, *s.a.* 420.

61. "melancholia": *al-sawdāʾ*. A state of sadness or depression brought on by an excess of black bile in the body. It is called *mālīkhūliyā* by Ibn Funduq, p. 47.

See also M. Levey and N. al-Khaledy, *The Medical Formulary of al-Samarqandī* (Philadelphia, 1967), p. 201.

62. "Shams al-Dawla": Abū Ṭāhir ibn Fakhr al-Dawla ᶜAlī, who became the the ruler of Hamadhān and Qirmīsīn upon the death of his father in 387/997. See Ibn al-Athīr, IX, 132, *s.a.* 387. According to Ibn al-Athīr, IX, 250–51, *s.a.* 405, Shams al-Dawla's attack on al-Rayy took place in 405/1015.

63. "Hilāl ibn Badr ibn Ḥasanūyah": Hilāl, Badr, and Ḥasanūyah (Ḥasanawayh) were Kurdish rulers of the area around Qirmīsīn, sometimes allied with one or another of the Būyids against other members of the family or outside rulers. See Ibn al-Athīr, IX, 5–8, *s.a.* 370, for an account of the struggles between Badr and ᶜAḍud al-Dawla in 370/980. Badr seems to have taken control of Qirmīsīn after the death of Fakhr al-Dawla in 387/997. Hilāl had been the prisoner of Sulṭān al-Dawla (d. 412/1021) in Baghdād, but he was released and given troops by Sulṭān al-Dawla after the latter found out about the death of Badr and the subsequent gains in territory by Shams al-Dawla. In a battle which took place in Dhū al-qaᶜda, 405/May, 1015, Hilāl was killed and the troops of Sulṭān al-Dawla were forced to return to Baghdād. See Ibn al-Athīr, IX, 248–49, *s.a.* 405; Miskawayh, *Tajārib al-umam*, ed. and trans. H. F. Amedroz and D.S. Margoliouth, with the continuations of Abū Shujāᶜ al-Rūdhrāwarī and Hilāl ibn al-Muḥassin, as *The Eclipse of the Abbasid Caliphate* (London, 1920–21), VI, 319 and 332, where the Caliph, al-Qādir (d. 422/1031) confirmed Badr in his territories in the Jibāl.

64. "events occurred": According to one later historian, Ibn Sīnā was forced to leave both Jurjān and al-Rayy by pressures placed on their rulers by Maḥmūd, who wanted them to send Ibn Sīnā to his court. See Ghiyāth al-Dīn Muḥammad, Khwāndamīr, *Tārīkh al-wuzarā*ᵓ, MS. John G. White Collection, Cleveland Public Library, fols. 63a and 63b. Usually this title is cited as *Dastūr al-wuzarā*ᵓ*:* see J. Rypka, *History of Iranian Literature* (Dordrecht, Holland, 1968), p. 454. The work was written ca. 915/1509–10.

65. "Qazwīn": A large city to the west of al-Rayy. See Yāqūt, *Buldān*, IV, 88–91; Le Strange, pp. 218–20.

66. "Hamadhān": written Hamadān by the Iranians. It was one of the four capitals of the Jibāl, and at this time it was, in theory at least, part of the domains of Majd al-Dawla, inherited from Fakhr al-Dawla, but Shams al-Dawla had been assigned the governorship of Hamadhān and Qirmīsīn (see above, n. 62). By the time of Ibn Sīnā's move to Hamadhān, Shams al-Dawla was obviously acting independently of orders from Majd al-Dawla or, more correctly, his mother, al-Sayyida. See Yāqūt, *Buldān*, IV, 981–92; Le Strange, pp. 194–95.

67. "Kādhabānūyah": Ibn Funduq, p. 47, gives the Persian form of this name: Kādbānūyah. None of the sources gives any further information about this person, nor is she mentioned in the standard biographical dictionaries. However, Kādbānū means a lady or matron in Persian, according to Steingass, *Persian-English Dictionary* (London, 1892), p. 1018. Since the Arabic equivalent of *kādbānū* is *al-sayyida*, and we know from other sources that Majd al-Dawla (and therefore his mother) had administrative and financial interests in Hamadhān—in Miskawayh, *Eclipse*, VI,

491, a certain Abū Saᶜd Muḥammad ibn Ismāᶜīl ibn al-Faḍl is said to be Majd al-Dawla's deputy in Hamadhān in 393/1003—is it possible that the affairs of Kādhabānūyah means the affairs of al-Sayyida?

68. "Qirmīsīn": also Qirmāsīn, the Arabic appellation of the city—one of the four capitals of the Jibāl—known to the Persians as Kirmānshāh or Kirmānshāhān. It lies to the west of Hamadhān, and at this time was being disputed by the Būyids and various Kurdish dynasties (see above, n. 63; also see below, n. 69). See also Yāqūt, *Buldān*, IV, 69–70; Le Strange, p. 187.

69. "ᶜAnnāz": Ḥusām al-Dīn Abū Shawk Fāris ibn Muḥammad ibn ᶜAnnāz, who ruled over parts of the Jibāl from 401/1010 to 437/1046. Abū Shawk probably took Qirmīsīn when Shams al-Dawla was attacking al-Rayy and fighting against Badr ibn Ḥasanūyah and Hilāl ibn Badr. The probable date for this attack on Abū Shawk was 406/1015. See Ibn al-Athīr, IX, 246, 248, and 531, *s.a.* 404, 405, and 437 (for the death of Abū Shawk); see also V. Minorsky, "ᶜAnnāzids," *EI*², I, 512.

70. "Shaykh Abū Saᶜd ibn Dakhdūl": Ibn Funduq, p. 48, and B give his *kunya* as Abū Saᶜīd, and N and Q / IAU give his patronymic as ibn Dakhdūk. His name does not appear in any of the standard biographical dictionaries, nor is either version of his name mentioned by F. Justi, *Iranisches Namenbuch* (Marburg, 1895).

71. "I would read ... the *Qānūn*": Ibn Funduq, p. 49, gives a more complete account: "Abū ᶜUbayd read from the *Shifā*ᵓ, al-Maᶜṣūmī from the *Qānūn*, [Ibn Zaylā from the *Instructions*, and Bahmanyār from *The Sum and Substance*]." But the bibliography states that the *Instructions* was the last work written by Ibn Sīnā (see above, pp. 96-97, so the latter two examples, not found in the earlier manuscripts of Ibn Funduq, seem to be false interpolations.

72. "al-Ṭārum": A large district in the mountains between Qazwīn and Jīlān with no well-known city in it. Yāqūt, *Buldān*, I, 811. Yāqūt spells the word Tāram, or Tarm, but the Arab geographers usually refer to it as al-Ṭārumayn, distinguishing between Upper Ṭārum, entirely in the Daylam territory, and Lower Ṭārum, further south and east, closer to Qazwīn and Hamadhān. Le Strange, pp. 225–26.

73. "its Amīr": In the year of Shams al-Dawla's death, 412/1021, the ruler of al-Ṭārum was probably a member of the family of Wahsūdān, the name of whose dynasty is variously known as the Musāfirids, Sallārids, or Kangarids (see Bosworth, *Dynasties*, p. 86). The strongest fortress in the Ṭārum district, Samīrān (or Shamīrān—see Le Strange, p. 226), had been taken from the young son of "Nūḥ ibn Wahsūdān" in 379/989 by Fakhr al-Dawla, who also married Nūḥ's widow. See Yāqūt, *Buldān*, III, 149.

After the death of Fakhr al-Dawla in 387/997, "Ibrāhīm ibn al-Marzubān ibn Ismāᶜīl ibn Wahsūdān . . . " seized a number of towns in the district of al-Ṭārum and was still in control of them when Maḥmūd of Ghazna invaded the Jibāl in 420/1029. See Ibn al-Athīr, IX, 373, *s.a.* 420.

Ibn Funduq, p. 49, Khwāndamīr, *Wuzarā*ᵓ, fol. 64a, and a later addition to J, read *al-amīr bahā*ᵓ *al-dawla*, instead of *al-amīr bihā*, but the Būyid Amīr Bahāᵓ al-Dawla Fīrūz had died in 403/1012, and he had never ruled in the Jibāl. See Bosworth, *Dynasties*, pp. 94–95; Ibn al-Athīr, IX, 241, *s.a.* 403.

74. "the son of Shams al-Dawla": Samāʾ al-Dawla Abū al-Ḥasan (ʿAlī, according to an addition to J) ibn Shams al-Dawla (r. 412/1028-before 421/1030). He ruled independently for two years, then he fell under the suzerainty of ʿAlāʾ al-Dawla in 414/1023 (see next note and n. 80). By the year 421/1030 ʿAlāʾ al-Dawla had appointed a deputy to govern Hamadhān and nothing is said of Samāʾ al-Dawla. See Ibn al-Athīr, IX, 395, *s.a.* 421.

75. "ʿAlāʾ al-Dawla": ʿAlāʾ al-Dawla Abū Jaʿfar Muḥammad ibn Dushmanziyār (Dushmanzār). He was called Ibn Kākūyah (or Ibn Kākawayh) because "he was the son of the maternal uncle of Majd al-Dawla and maternal uncle (*al-khāl*) in their language is *kākūyah*." Ibn al-Athīr, IX, 495, *s.a.* 433. But earlier Ibn al-Athīr, IX, 207, *s.a.* 398, had stated that "he was the son of the maternal uncle of Majd al-Dawla's mother." Bosworth, *Dynasties*, p. 97, says that "Muḥammad was the Būyid Amīr Majd al-Dawla's maternal uncle, " but since he is usually referred to as Ibn Kākūyah or *pisar-i kākū* (Persian for the son of the kākū), Bosworth's statement must be an error, which should correctly read, "Muḥammad was *the son of* the Būyid Amīr Majd al-Dawla's maternal uncle." See Abū al-Faḍl Muḥammad ibn Ḥusayn Bayhaqī, *Tārīkh-i Masʿūdī*, ed. Q. Ghanī and ʿA.A. Fayyāḍ (Teheran, 1324/1945), pp. 15–17, for references to *pisar-i kākū*.

But the question remains: who was the maternal uncle of whom? Two other figures appear on the scene to complicate the issue, a certain al-Marzubān and his son Rustam. Ibn al-Athīr, IX, 141, *s.a.* 388, states that al-Marzubān was the maternal uncle of Majd al-Dawla, but earlier he had referred to "Rustam ibn al-Marzubān, the maternal uncle of Majd al-Dawla," p. 140, where either of the two men could be his maternal uncle.

This appellation—Rustam ibn al-Marzubān, the maternal uncle of Majd al-Dawla—appears also in Ẓahīr al-Dīn Marʿashī, *Ṭārīkh-i Tabaristān wa Rūyān wa Māzandarān*, ed. M. H. Tasbīḥī (Teheran, 1345/1966), pp. 82, 95. Rustam-i Marzubān, the maternal uncle of Majd al-Dawla, is mentioned by Mīrkhwānd : see Mirkhond, *Histoire des Samanides*, ed. and trans. Charles Defrémery (Paris, 1845), pp. 101 (text), and 212 (trans.). But on page 85 of Marʿashī's work, Rustam is specifically called the maternal uncle of Majd al-Dawla. So it would seem that the evidence points to Rustam, rather than his father, al-Marzubān, who was the brother of al-Sayyida and the uncle of Majd al-Dawla.

Another problem arises when one tries to separate proper names from titles; both *marzubān* and *dushmanziyār* (or *dushmanzār*) may be descriptive or honorific titles, the first meaning a margrave or lord-marcher and the second meaning one who brings grief (*zār*) to his enemy (*dushman*). Was Dushmanziyār the same person as Rustam, or did al-Sayyida have two brothers, Dushmanziyār and Rustam? Eduard von Zambaur, *Manuel de généalogie et de chronologie pour l'histoire de l'Islam* (Hanovre, 1927), pp. 216-17, says that Rustam and Dushmanzār (not Dushmanziyār, as in Ibn al-Athīr) were one and the same person and that he was al-Sayyida's brother. However, it would seem that al-Sayyida had two brothers, based on two pieces of evidence found in Miskawayh and Ibn al-Athīr.

In 392 [1002], according to Miskawayh, *Eclipse*, VI, 477, or in 393 [1003], according to Ibn al-Athīr, IX, 178, Abū al-ʿAbbās al-Ḍabbī, the wazīr of Majd al-Dawla, fled to Badr ibn Ḥasanūyah for protection. al-Sayyida suspected him of poisoning the "elder Iṣpahbud," whom Miskawayh calls al-Sayyida's nephew. Ibn al-Athīr, however, says that he was her brother (though for some reason he uses the masculine possessive pronoun: *akhāhu*, rather than *akhāhā*). Although the "elder Iṣpahbud" could have been the father of an implied "younger Iṣpahbud," the possibility of the two men being brothers of al-Sayyida is increased by a further piece of evidence provided by Ibn al-Athīr.

He reports (IX, 351-52) that in 417 [1026] ʿAlāʾ al-Dawla appointed two of his cousins to administrative or military posts. Their names were Abū Jaʿfar, the elder of the two, and Abū Manṣūr, who are called "the two sons of his paternal uncle (*abnā ʿammihi*)." See also Zambaur, *Manuel*, p. 217.

Zambaur, pp. 187, 216, also states that al-Marzubān al-Daylamī was related to the Bāwandid family, which had ruled in the Caspian coastlands of Ṭabaristān since before the arrival of Islam, but Bosworth, *The Ghaznavids* (Edinburgh, 1963), p. 74, says that this claim, made by the Kākūyids, is a false one, and it is certainly not put forward in Ibn al-Athīr or Marʿashī.

For a different set of conclusions drawn from the same evidence, see Bosworth, "Dailamīs in Central Iran: the Kākūyids of Jibāl and Yazd," *Iran*, VII (1970), 73–95, especially pp. 73–74 and the genealogical table on p. 95. Bosworth, e.g., says that Rustam and Dushmanziyār were the same person (p. 73); he calls Rustam the maternal uncle of al-Sayyida (p. 74); and says, therefore, that al-Sayyida was ʿAlāʾ al-Dawla's first cousin, not nephew [*sic*, but presumably meaning aunt]. For a genealogical table which exhibits the conclusions I have drawn from the above data, see below.

ʿAlāʾ al-Dawla was appointed governor of Iṣfahān by al-Sayyida in 398/1008, and remained in power there and in other parts of the Jibāl, except when driven out temporarily by Sulṭān Masʿūd ibn Maḥmūd or his lieutenants, until his death in 433/1041. He was a patron of scholars, and Ibn Funduq, p. 50, says that it was he who initiated the correspondence and asked Ibn Sīnā to come to his court after the death of Shams al-Dawla.

Genealogical Table of the Kākūyids
(Bāwandids?)

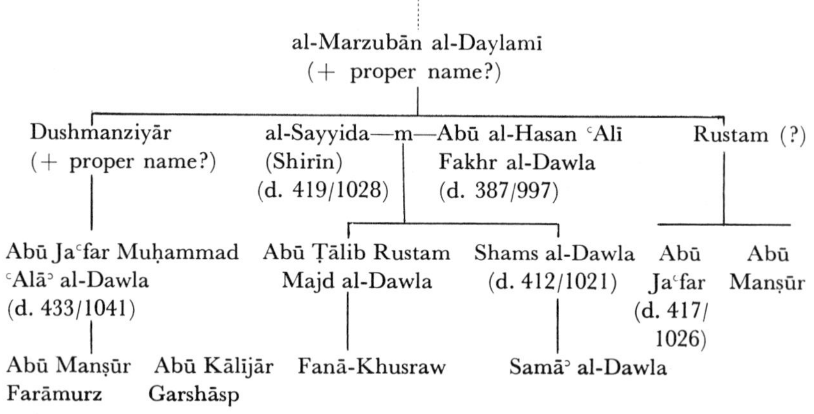

76. "Abū Ghālib the Druggist": *al-ᶜaṭṭār*. None of the standard biographical dictionaries mention his name.

77. "he had finished all . . . Animals": The *Shifāʾ*, written over a period of years, beginning ca. 406/1015 and finished probably ca. 423/1032, contains the following parts: Part I, "Logic," divided into nine sections (*Isagoge*, Categories, Hermeneutics, Analytics, Apodictics, Topics, Sophistics, Rhetoric, and Poetics); Part II, "Physics," divided into eight sections (Scope of Physics, the Heavens and the Earth, Generation and Corruption, the Active and Passive, Inanimate Beings, Psychology or the Soul, Plants, and Animals); Part III, "Mathematics," divided into four sections (Euclid or Geometry, Arithmetic, Music, and Astronomy or the Almagest); and Part IV, "Metaphysics."

78. "Tāj al-Mulk": Abū Naṣr ibn Bahrām. Ibn al-Athīr, IX, 320, *s.a.* 411, says that he was the wazīr of Shams al-Dawla, presumably having replaced Ibn Sīnā in that position. In a battle which took place in Hamadhān in 411/1020, between the Kurdish and Turkish troops of Shams al-Dawla, Tāj al-Mulk was the leader of the Kurdish forces. Although he called in ᶜAlāʾ al-Dawla for aid in defeating the Turkish troops, three years later he led the forces opposing ᶜAlāʾ al-Dawla (see below, n. 80). There, in Ibn al-Athīr, IX, 330, *s.a.* 414, he is called *al-Qūhī*, the Mountaineer, or the Kurd. The *Durrat al-akhbār*, a Persian translation of Ibn Funduq made in the 8th/14th century, calls Tāj al-Mulk the brother of Samāʾ al-Dawla and therefore the son of Shams al-Dawla. See *Durrat al-akhbār*, ed. M. Shafīᶜ as Vol. II of the *Tatimmat Ṣiwān al-ḥikma* (Lahore, 1935), p. 42.

79. "Fardajān": According to Yāqūt, *Buldān*, III, 870, Fardajān is a well-known castle of Hamadhān in the district of Jarrā. It is also known as Barahān or Bardahān. Ibn al-Athīr, IX, 403, *s.a.* 421, says that it is fifteen *farsakhs* (about fifty-five miles) from Hamadhān. Ibn Funduq, p. 50, gives the name of this castle as Nardawān.

80. "ᶜAlāʾ al-Dawla ... seized it": ᶜAlāʾ al-Dawla attacked Hamadhān and defeated the forces of Samāʾ al-Dawla and Tāj al-Mulk in the year 414/1023. See Ibn al-Athīr, IX, 330-31, *s.a.* 414.

81. "the son of Shams al-Dawla": All of the manuscripts give this reading: Tāj al-Mulk ibn Shams al-Dawla, rather than Tāj al-Mulk *wa* Ibn Shams al-Dawla. Ibn al-Athīr, IX, 331, *s.a.* 414, states that only Tāj al-Mulk was in the castle, Samāʾ al-Dawla having already submitted to ᶜAlāʾ al-Dawla. The reading in the manuscripts, then, would agree with the statement in the *Durrat al-akhbār* (see above, n. 78) that Tāj al-Mulk and Samāʾ al-Dawla were brothers.

82. "the ᶜAlid": *al-ᶜAlawī*. This term is used as a *nisba* by Shīᶜites of both the Ismāᶜīlī and Twelver branches. See, e.g., Ibn al-Athīr, IX, 329, 364, 411, 460, *s.a.* 413, 418, 421, 429, for obituary notices of a number of people with this *nisba*. No information on this person is found in the standard biographical dictionaries. However, one of the works which Ibn Sīnā wrote in Hamadhān, *Cardiac Remedies*, is dedicated to "al-Sharīf al-Saᶜīd Abū al-Ḥusayn ᶜAlī ibn al-Ḥusayn ibn al-Ḥasanī" (Mahdavi, p. 24), whose name would imply strongly that he was a Shīᶜite.

83. "Iṣfahān": One of the four capitals of the Jibāl, lying to the southeast of

Hamadhān, it is also spelled Iṣbahān or Iṣpahān. See Yāqūt, *Buldān*, I, 292–98; Le Strange, pp. 202–7.

84. "Ṭihrān": All the sources but J read Ṭabarān, which is incorrect, since the only Ṭabarān given by the geographers is one of the twin towns which made up the city of Ṭūs, in Khurāsān. See Yāqūt, *Buldān*, III, 486, for Ṭabarān, and I, 293, where he lists the *rustaqs* of Iṣfahān, with Ṭabarān not occurring there. Two other spellings are possible:

(1) Ṭabarak, combining a word for mountain with the diminutive suffix, *-ak*, with the meaning, therefore, of hillock. There was a fortress by this name at al-Rayy, and according to Le Strange, p. 205, there was a citadel by this name in Iṣfahān at the time of Tīmūr's conquest, at the end of the 8th/14th century. See Ibn al-Athīr, IX, 131, *s.a.* 387, for the fortress of "Ṭabaraq," where Fakhr al-Dawla died. See also Yāqūt, *Buldān*, III, 507-08.

(2) Ṭihrān, which Yāqūt, *Buldān*, III, 565, and Ḥamd Allāh Mustawfī al-Qazwīnī list as one of the districts of Iṣfahān. See *Nuzhat al-qulūb*, Geographical Section, ed. and trans. G. Le Strange, Gibb Memorial Series, XXIII (London and Leiden, 1913–15), Vol. I (edition), 50, and Vol. II (translation), 57. Although only one manuscript gives this reading, it must be the correct one. The other copyists misread the word as Ṭabarān because that city was well known, whereas Ṭihrān, as a district of Iṣfahān, would have been known to very few people.

85. "Kūy Kunbadh": the quarter, or district, of the dome. See Steingass, *Persian-English Dictionary*, p. 1065, for the meaning of *kūy* as quarter or district. This quarter of Iṣfahān is not mentioned by Yāqūt or Mustawfī, but it occurs as Kūy Gunbad in the *Chahār maqāla*, p. 64, and it is translated by Browne as "Gate of the Dome." It also appears as Kūy Kunbadh (Gunbad) in the *Durrat al-akhbār*, p. 43, and in J. All of the other manuscripts read Kūn Kunbadh. See E. G. Browne, trans., *Chahār maqāla*, by Niẓāmī ʿArūḍī Samarqandī (London, 1900), p. 103.

86, "ʿAbd Allāh ibn Bībī": There is no mention of this person in any of the standard biographical dictionaries.

87. "Almagest ... Euclid": See above, nn. 20, 21. Ibn Khaldūn, *Muqaddima*, p. 488, trans., III, 135, says of the Almagest, "the leading Islamic philosophers [*ḥukamāʾ*] have abridged it; thus Ibn Sīnā did it and inserted it in the teachings of the *Shifāʾ*."

In the same fashion, he says of the Euclid, p. 486, trans., III, 130, "people have made many abridgements of it; e.g., Ibn Sīna did it in the teachings of the *Shifāʾ*, where he inserted a part of it which he had selected for it."

88. "geometrical figures": *shubahāʾ*. For this usage, see R. Dozy, *Supplement aux dictionnaires arabes* (Leiden, 1881; rpt. Beirut, 1968), I, 726. Also see al-Khwārazmī, *Mafātīḥ*, p. 206.

89. "in the year ... attacked Sābūr Khwāst": ʿAlāʾ al-Dawla attacked Sābūr Khwast a number of times, according to Ibn al-Athīr. After his attack on Hamadhān in 414/1023, he went on to conquer Sābūr Khwāst. See Ibn al-Athīr, IX, 331, *s.a.* 414. But Ibn Sīnā was not yet in Iṣfahān, so this could not have been the date of

the completion of the *Shifā*ᵓ. ᶜAlāᵓ al-Dawla made other attacks on Sābūr Khwāst in 417/1026 and 421/1030, based on inferences from Ibn al-Athīr, IX, 351–52, *s.a.* 417, and 402, *s.a.* 421.

Since al-Jūzjānī states in his introduction to the *Shifā*ᵓ (Mahdavi, p. 129) that Ibn Sīnā was forty years old when he finished the work, the latter campaign mentioned above (in 421/1030) is probably the one referred to by al-Jūzjānī in the biography. The *Najāt* may have been written during this campaign, or perhaps a later one; Ibn al-Athīr, IX, 424, *s.a.* 423, specifically places ᶜAlāᵓ al-Dawla in Sābūr Khwāst in 423/1032.

Sābūr Khwāst, written by the Persians Shāpūr Khwāst, was a city in a province of the same name, lying to the south of Hamadhān and to the west of Iṣfahān. At different times during this period it was under the control of Shams al-Dawla, Abū Shawk Fāris, the ᶜAnnāzid, and ᶜAlāᵓ al-Dawla. See Yāqūt, *Buldān*, III, 4–5; Le Strange, pp. 200–2.

90. "great number of journeys ... errors" : It is difficult to say whether al-Jūzjānī means the great number of journeys taken by the observers who compiled these tables, or of the travels through many hands which the tables themselves made. Ibn Khaldūn, in discussing the fate of astronomical observations in Islam, says, *Muqaddima*, p. 488, trans., III, 134, "in Islam, only a little concern has been paid to it, much of which was in the days of al-Maᵓmūn [r. 198/813–218/833], who made a well-known instrument for observation called an armillary sphere—he started it but he did not finish it—and when he died traces of it [his observations] disappeared and were forgotten. Those who followed depended upon the ancient observations, but these were useless because of the change of the movements (*li'khtilāf al-ḥarakāt*) in the course of time."

Ibn Funduq, p. 52, says the cause was the great number of journeys and the accumulation (*tarākum*) of errors.

Another possibility is that suggested by Aydin Sayili, *The Observatory in Islam*, Publications of the Turkish Historical Society, Series VIII, No. 38 (Ankara, 1960), p. 156, where he translates this passage as "because of many journeys undertaken and due to certain other obstacles the activity of observation was interrupted." This however, seems to be too loose a translation; *al-khalal* can hardly mean interruptions, and they had already been referred to as being present in the ephemerides of the ancients.

91. "the *ᶜAlāᵓī*": A work in Persian similar to the *Najāt*, called today the *Dānishnāmah-yi ᶜAlāᵓi*, or *Book of Knowledge of ᶜAlā*ᵓ [al-Dawla].

92. "twenty-five years": Ibn Funduq, p. 52, says that Abū ᶜUbayd was the friend and pupil of Ibn Sīnā for thirty years, but this must be inaccurate, since in his introduction to the *Shifā*ᵓ, al-Jūzjānī states, "I met him when he was in Jurjān, when he was about thirty-two years old." See Mahdavi, p. 128. Since the two men met shortly after the death of Qābūs, which occurred in 403/1013, and Ibn Sīnā died in 428/1037, at age fifty-eight, twenty-five years would be the correct figure.

93. "Abū Manṣūr al-Jabbān": Muḥammad ibn ᶜAlī ibn ᶜUmar Abū Manṣūr al-Jabbān was his full name, according to Yāqūt, *Irshād*, VII, 45–46. al-Samᶜānī,

Ansāb, fols. 120b–121a, explains that the *nisba*, al-Jabbān, is given to one who learns correct Arabic usage from the Bedouin in the desert—*al-jabbāna*, according to al-Samᶜānī, is a word which means desert.

Abū Manṣūr, according to Yāqūt, was a member of the entourage of al-Ṣāḥib ibn ᶜAbbād (see below, n. 97), but he became estranged from him before the Ṣāḥib's death in 385/995. He remained in al-Rayy, however, until 416/1025, when he went to Iṣfahān and the court of ᶜAlāʾ al-Dawla.

94. "Abū Manṣūr al-Azharī": Muḥammad ibn Aḥmad ibn al-Azhar ibn Ṭalḥa Abū Manṣūr al-Azharī al-Harawī was born in Harāt in 282/895 and died, apparently in the same city, in 370/980, the year of Ibn Sīnā's birth. He studied philology in Harāt and Baghdād and spent two years as a prisoner of a Bedouin tribe in Baḥrayn, where he studied their very pure Arabic. He wrote a number of works on lexicography. See Yāqūt, *Irshād*, VI, 197–99; see also *GAL*, I, 129, and *GAL*, *S*, I, 197; and R. Blachère, "al-Azharī," *EI*², I, 822. al-Samᶜānī, *Ansāb*, fols. 28b–29a, does not list Abū Manṣūr.

The *Correct Philology* (recently edited and published in Cairo) is arranged in the manner of al-Khalīl's *Kitāb al-ᶜayn*, with the roots classified phonetically, not alphabetically. Much of this work by Abū Manṣūr was used by Ibn Manẓūr in his *Lisān al-ᶜarab*. See J. A. Haywood, *Arabic Lexicography*, 2nd ed. (Leiden, 1965), pp. 20–40 (on al-Khalīl), 77–82 (on Ibn Manẓūr).

95. "Ibn al-ᶜAmīd": Abū al-Faḍl Muḥammad ibn al-ᶜAmīd Abī ᶜAbd Allāh ibn al-Ḥusayn, al-Kātib, was appointed wazīr in 328/940 by Rukn al-Dawla (r. 335/947–366/977) and was called the second Jāḥiẓ, because of his epistolary style. He died in 359–60/969–70. See *GAL*, *S*, I, 153; see also C. Cahen, "Ibn al-ᶜAmīd," *EI*², III, 703–04; al-Thaᶜālibī, *Yatīma*, III, 158–85.

96. "al-Ṣābī": Abū Isḥāq Ibrāhīm ibn Hilāl ibn Ibrāhīm al-Ḥarrānī, al-Ṣābī (313/925–384/994) was in the chancery of Muᶜizz al-Dawla (r. 334/945–356/967) and was known as a great prose stylist. See *GAL*, I, 96, and *GAL*, *S*, I, 153–54; F. Krenkow, "al-Ṣābī," *Encyclopaedia of Islam* (Leiden, 1913–42), IV, 19–20; Ibn al-Athīr, IX, 106, *s.a.* 384, for the notice of his death; al-Thaᶜālibī, *Yatīma*, II, 242–312, for examples of his style.

97. "al-Ṣāḥib": Abū al-Qāsim Ismāᶜīl ibn ᶜAbbād ibn al-ᶜAbbās, al-Ṣāḥib, al-Ṭalqānī (324–26/936–38–385/995) was the wazīr of Muʾayyid al–Dawla (r. 366/977–373/983) and his son, Fakhr al-Dawla, in al-Rayy. A brilliant writer and administrator, he was a patron of both Arabic and Persian writers. See *GAL*, I, 130–31, and *GAL*, *S*, I, 198–99; al-Samᶜānī, *Ansāb*, fol. 363a; al-Thaᶜālibī, *Yatīma*, III, 192–290; C. Cahen and C. Pellat, "Ibn ᶜAbbād," *EI*², III, 671–73; Muḥammad ᶜAufī, *Lubāb al-albāb*, ed. E.G. Browne and M. Qazwīnī, 2 vols. (London and Leiden, 1903–06), Vol, II, 16–19.

98. "rose preserve . . . sugar": Some of the manuscripts (A and B) have *sakanjubīn al-sukkar*, sugar oxymel—i.e., oxymel made with sugar rather than honey, which the Greeks necessarily used. See Levey and al-Khaledy, *Medical Formulary*, p. 62, for a definition of oxymel, and p. 172, n. 25: ". . . Ibn Sīnā found it [oxymel] useful for the stomach. . . ." See also al-Khwārazmī, *Māfātīḥ*, pp. 175–76: "*jalanjabīn* is composed of rose and honey, *sakanjubīn* is made of vinegar and honey and given this

name, but if sugar is used in place of honey and syrup of quince or something else in place of vinegar the confections are called preserves (*al-anbijāt*)."

99 "*manns*": One *mann* (or *manā*) is said by al-Khwārazmī, *Mafātīḥ*, p. 14, to have the weight of two *ratls*, or 257 *dirhams*. The weight of one *dirham* is variously given by modern scholars. See G. C. Miles, "Dirham," *EI*², II, 319.

100 "Shīrāz": The capital of the province of Fārs, south of Iṣfahān. See Yāqūt, *Buldān*, III, 348–50; Le Strange, pp. 249–52.

101. "Abū al-Qāsim al-Kirmānī": Ibn Funduq, pp. 32–33, says that Ibn Sīnā and Abū al-Qāsim quarreled bitterly, exchanging a number of insults. Abū al-Qāsim is not listed in al-Samᶜānī, *Ansāb*, fol. 480a, or Yāqūt, *Irshād*.

102. "Ibrāhīm ibn Bābā al-Daylamī": He is not listed in the standard biographical dictionaries.

103. "esoteric interpretation": *ᶜilm al-bāṭin*. Meaning that he was a Shīᶜite, or perhaps a Ṣūfī, since these two groups argued for an esoteric as well as an exoteric (*al-ẓāhir*) interpretation of the Qurᵓān. The name, or rather title, Bābā would imply a Ṣūfī background, since this term, like Shaykh or Pīr, meant the leader of a group of Ṣūfīs. See M. G. S. Hodgson, "Bāṭiniyya," *EI*², I, 1098–1100.

104. "Firᶜawnī": This is a designation of one of the early types of paper used in the Muslim world; it is listed by Ibn al-Nadīm, *Fihrist*, I, 21. See also C. Huart, "Kāghad," *EI*¹, II, 624; also see Huart, *Les calligraphes et miniaturistes de l'Orient musulman* (Paris, 1908), p. 9.

105. "Sulṭān Masᶜūd": Shibhā al-Dawla Abū Saᶜīd Masᶜūd ibn Maḥmūd (r. 421/1031–432/1041), Ghaznavid Sulṭān who replaced his father after a brief attempt by his brother Muḥammad to take control. He ruled over the Ghaznavid Empire at its greatest extent, but he was also the Sulṭān who saw the beginnings of its dissolution—the Saljuq conquest of Khwārazm and Khurāsān. See Bosworth, *Ghaznavids*, ch. VIII, pp. 227–40.

106. "on the day when . . . not found afterwards": Masᶜūd had been appointed governor of the Jibāl by Maḥmūd soon after the latter's conquest of al-Rayy and his return to Khurāsān. Masᶜūd then attacked Iṣfahān and took the city from ᶜAlāᵓ al-Dawla; upon his return to al-Rayy, the people of Iṣfahān rebelled against his deputies there and he had to return to put down the rebellion, killing about five thousand people, according to Ibn al-Athīr, IX, 372, *s.a.* 420.

Yet ᶜAlāᵓ al-Dawla was in Iṣfahān the following year, according to Ibn al-Athīr, IX, 395, *s.a.* 421, but was driven out by a deputy of Masᶜūd, sent from al-Rayy. It was while ᶜAlāᵓ al-Dawla was in exile at Tustar, in Khūzistān, southwest of Iṣfahan asking aid from its ruler, the Būyid Abū Kālījār (d. 440/1048), that the news of Maḥmūd's death came to him, and he realized that Masᶜūd must return to Ghazna. And so ᶜAlāᵓ al-Dawla returned to Iṣfahān and took that city, Hamadhān, and al-Rayy from the troops of Masᶜūd. See Ibn al-Athīr, IX, 395, 402, *s.a.* 412; see also Gardīzī, *Zayn*, p. 194.

However, the sack of Iṣfahān referred to here by al-Jūzjānī was probably not any of those which took place in 420 and 421, but rather an attack which took place in 425/1034. The forces of Masʿūd were led by Abū Sahl al-Ḥamdūnī, or al-Ḥamdawī, in al-Thaʿālibī, *Tatimmat al-Yatīma*, ed. ʿA. Iqbāl (Teheran, 1353/1934), II, 60. According to Ibn al-Athīr, IX, 436, *s.a.* 425, after Abū Sahl had defeated ʿAlāʾ al-Dawla, "he pillaged the treasuries and goods of ʿAlāʾ al-Dawla; and the books of Abū ʿAlī Ibn Sīnā, who was in the service of ʿAlāʾ al-Dawla, were seized and carried to Ghazna and put in the libraries there, until the troops of al-Ḥusayn ibn al-Ḥusayn al-Ghūrī burned it. . . ." The destruction of Ghazna was carried out by the troops of ʿAlāʾ al-Dīn al-Ḥusayn, Jahān-sūz (World-Incendiary) in 545/1150–51. See Bosworth, "The Political and Dynastic History of the Iranian World (A.D. 1000–1217)," *The Cambridge History of Iran*, Vol. V, *The Saljuq and Mongol Periods*, ed. J.A. Boyle (Cambridge, 1968), p. 160.

Ibn Funduq, p. 56, reporting on the loss of the *Judgment*, says that a certain ʿAzīz al-Dīn al-Faqāʿī al-Riḥānī claimed, "in 545 I bought a copy of it in Iṣfahān and took it to Marw." Ibn Funduq also adds at this poit that *Eastern Philosophy* and *Throne Philosophy* (see above, pp. 102–03 and 104–05) were also in the Ghaznavid libraries which were destroyed by the Ghūrid ruler.

107. "concupiscible faculties": *al-quwā al-shahwāniyya*. One of the two branches of the appetitive faculty (*al-quwwat al-shawqiyya*), it is that faculty "which induces [a person] to move, by which [movement] he approaches the things which seem necessary or useful, in pursuit of sensual pleasure." *Najāt*, p. 259, quoted by Goichon, *Lexique*, p. 334. This faculty is the Latin *vis concupiscibilis*.

108. "Tāsh Farrāsh": One of the army commanders and governors of both Maḥmūd and Masʿūd, he is called al-Amīr Ḥusām al-Dawla Abū al-ʿAbbās Tāsh Farrāsh by Ibn Funduq, p. 57. But Ibn Funduq has confused him with an earlier figure, the Ḥājib Tāsh, who was given the command of the army of Khurāsān by the Sāmānid, Nūḥ ibn Manṣūr (see above, n. 3), who also gave him the *laqab* (honorific title) of Ḥusām al-Dawla. See Gardīzī, *Zayn*, p. 166. They could not be the same person, because Gardīzī, p. 167, says that the Ḥājib Tāsh died in 378/988 (Ibn al-Athīr, IX, 29, *s.a.* 377, says the previous year.)

Tāsh Farrāsh was named governor of al-Rayy, Hamadhān, and the Jibāl by Masʿūd in 422/1031, but he was replaced by Abū Sahl al-Ḥamdūnī (al-Ḥamdawī) in 424/1033, because of his oppression of the people of al-Rayy and the Jibāl. See Ibn al-Athīr, IX, 421, 428–29, *s.a.* 421, 424. Tāsh Farrāsh, however, remained in the Jibāl and was commanding troops under Abū Sahl as late as 427/1036. See Ibn al-Athīr, IX, 380, *s.a.* 420.

The year in which Tāsh Farrāsh fought against ʿAlāʾ al-Dawla at Karaj, followed by ʿAlāʾ al-Dawla's retreat to Īdhaj, etc., as described by al-Jūzjānī, was probably 425/1034, since Ibn al-Athīr, IX, 435–36, *s.a.* 425, mentions essentially the same events as does al-Jūzjānī. This was the same attack in which Ibn Sīnā's books were taken (see above, n. 106).

It is possible, too, that this battle took place in 427/1036, although Ibn al-Athīr, IX, 446–47, *s.a.* 427, reports that Abū Sahl himself was leading the troops and that the battle with ʿAlāʾ al-Dawla took place near Iṣfahān. The outcome was the same—ʿAlāʾ al-Dawla's forces were routed—but this time they moved north looking for asylum. They asked the son of the Salār (*ibn al-Salār* = Justān II ibn Ibrāhīm?)

but were turned down and had to leave. See Bosworth, *Dynasties*, p. 86, for the Sallārid dynasty.

109. "al-Karaj": Most of the sources read al-Karkh, but this is certainly an error due to the very close resemblance of the name of this city in the area of Hamadhān to the name of the famous quarter of Baghdād, al-Karkh. Yāqūt, *Buldān*, IV, 988, says, "the district of Hamadān comprises 660 villages . . . from the gate of al-Karaj to Sīsar in length . . ." For al-Karkh, see Le Strange, pp. 31, 67; for al-Karaj, see Le Strange, p. 197. See also V. Minorsky, tr., *Ḥudūd al-ālam*, 2nd ed., ed. Bosworth, Gibb Memorial Series, New Series, XI (London, 1970), p. 132, where a copyist has made a similar mistake, calling Abū Dulaf of Karaj, Karkhī.

110. "Īdhaj": The name of a district and a town south of Iṣfahān, between that city and Khūzistān. At this time it was under the control of the Būyid ruler, Abū Kālījār (see above, n. 106). See Yāqūt, *Buldān*, I, 416-17; Le Strange, p. 245.

111. "two *dānaqs*": One *dānaq* theoretically equals one-sixth of a *dirham*. See Miles, "Dirham," *EI*², 319. But al-Khwārazmī, *Mafātīḥ*, pp. 62-63, states that one *dānaq* equals one-sixth of a *dīnār*, and since the *dirham* was seven-tenths of the *dīnār* in weight, one *dānaq* in this system would equal ten-forty-seconds of a *dirham*, slightly less than one-quarter. In either case, the doctor treating Ibn Sīnā put in ten to fifteen times the amount of celery seed prescribed.

112. "mithridate": *mithrūdhīṭūs*. An electuary named after Mithridates of Pontus (d. 63 B.C.), taken as a paste or sweet, usually containing opium. See al-Qifṭī, p. 324; see also Lane, *Lexicon*, I, pt. V, p. 1968, under *maᶜjūn*, electuary.

113. "he passed away . . . in the year 428": All of the sources, including Ibn Funduq, p. 58, except Ibn al-Athīr give the place of Ibn Sīnā's death and burial as Hamadhān; Ibn al-Athīr IX, 456, *s.a.* 428, says it was in Iṣfahān. al-Juzjani does not mention the exact day of Ibn Sīnā's death, but Ibn Funduq, p. 58, gives it as the first Friday of Ramaḍān, 428 / 18 June 1037. Ibn al-Athīr, IX, 456, *s.a.* 428, says that he died in Shaᶜbān, 428 / May–June 1037.

Ibn Abī Uṣaybiᶜa, II, 9, says that some say he was taken to Iṣfahān and buried there in the quarter where he had lived, Kūy Kunbadh (but spelled Kūn Kunbad, as before.)

114. "the year of his birth was 370": Most of the sources give the year 370/[980], with Ibn Funduq, p. 39, specifying the month of Ṣafar / August-September (see above, n. 8). However, Ibn Abī Uṣaybiᶜa, II, 9, says 375 /[985], but since no other source has this date, and since al-Jūzjānī's introduction to the *Shifāʾ* gives quite different information, supporting the date 370 / 980 (see above, n. 92), Ibn Abī Uṣaybiᶜa is clearly incorrect in this date. Khwāndamīr, *Wuzarāʾ*, fol. 66a, says that the year of his birth was 373/[983] and that his age at his death in 428/[1037] was sixty-three solar years and seven months. This is obviously an error, but if you assume that he meant fifty-three solar years and some months, it would be correct, but it would still place Ibn Sīnā's birth later than do all but one of the other sources.

Ibn Sīnā's age at his death, then, was 58 lunar years and some months, although Ibn Funduq, p. 59, says that his age was "*nḥ*" (58) *solar* years. His age in solar years, however, must have been 56 and 10 months.

NOTES TO THE TRANSLATION OF THE BIBLIOGRAPHY

1. "I have endeavored ... ninety works": The person who compiled this longer bibliography is unknown.

2. "Philosophy": *ḥikma.* This term is found instead of *falsafa*, which included only those subjects dealt with by the Greeks. The word "*falsafa*" does not occur in the bibliography, so I have translated *ḥikma* as "philosophy" throughout, although "wisdom" would be its more usual translation.

3. "for him in Jurjān": Ibn Abī Uṣaybiʿa's text adds, "I found in the front of the work that he wrote it for the Shaykh Abū Aḥmad Muḥammad ibn Ibrāhīm al-Fārisī." No notice of this person is given in the standard biographical dictionaries. Could this be the same person who is called Abū Muḥammad al-Shīrāzī in the text of the autobiography, or could this dedication possibly be to a son (or other relative) of Abū Muḥammad al-Shīrāzī?

4. "his brother ʿAlī": His brother is called Maḥmūd by Ibn Funduq, but his name is given as ʿAlī also in one of the verses of his Ode on logic, written when Ibn Sīnā was in Gurgānj. See Ibn Funduq p. 39; Mahdavi, p. 28.

5. "Abū Sahl al-Masīḥī ... in Jurjan": This statement placing the composition of this work in Jurjan contradicts the story told in the *Chahār maqāla*, which says that Abū Sahl died while accompanying Ibn Sīnā on his flight from Gurgānj to Jurjān. See above, Notes to the Translation of the Autobiography, n. 43.

6. "*Natural Faculties*": This is the title of an essay written by Abū al-Faraj ʿAbd Allāh ibn al-Ṭayyib al-Jāthlīq (d. 435/1043), a Christian physician of Baghdad who practiced in the hospital established by ʿAḍud al-Dawla (r. 367/978–372/983) in 372/982. See D. M. Dunlop, "Bīmāristān," *EI*^{2}, I, 1223. This work by Ibn Sīnā may be a commentary on Abū al-Faraj's work, which is listed by Ibn Abī Uṣaybiʿa, I, 241, and *GAL, S*, I, 884.

7. "Abū Saʿīd al-Yamāmī": He was a physician and author of works on medicine, whose full name is given by Ibn Abī Uṣaybiʿa, I, 240, as Abū Saʿīd al-Faḍl ibn ʿĪsā al-Yamāmī. He is mentioned as one of the teachers of Ibn Sīnā by Ibn Abī Uṣaybiʿa, *ibid.* Samʿānī, fol. 602a, does not list Abū Saʿīd, but does tell of the migration of the family from Yamāma in the Arabian Peninsula, first to Baṣra, and then to Baghdād, and notes that one of the members of the family studied in Iṣfahān. See also al-Qifṭī, p. 407.

8. "refuting ... *Faculties*": Is this work the same as No. 23 in this bibliography? Mahdavi, p. 116, believes that the two works are identical.

9. "flight to Iṣfahān": Although Ibn Sīnā's escape from Hamadhān and flight to Iṣfahān, which took place *ca.* 414/1023, would seem to be the one referred to

here, one of the MSS in Istanbul gives the date as the end of Muḥarram, 424/January, 1033. This would place its composition during ᶜAlāᵓ al-Dawla's flight from Tāsh Farrāsh, Sulṭān Masᶜūd's army commander, which is described in the biography of Ibn Sīnā and reported by Ibn al-Athīr, IX, 425, *s.a.* 423. See Mahdavi, p. 197, for a description of the MS.

10. "Ibn Zaylā": Abū Manṣūr al-Ḥusayn ibn Ṭāhir ibn Zaylā (or Ibn Zīla, according to Ibn Funduq) was one of Ibn Sīnā's favorite pupils. He was a native of Iṣfahān and may have been a Zoroastrian (Mājūsī); his fields of special competance were mathematics and music. He wrote several commentaries, including one on *Ḥayy ibn Yaqẓān*, and a book on the *Soul* (*al-nafs*). He died in 440/1048–49 at an early age. See Ibn Funḍuq, pp. 92–93.

11. "Bahmanyār": He is called Abū al-Ḥasan Bahmanyār ibn (al-) Marzubān by both Ibn Abī Uṣaybīᶜa, II, 19, and Ibn Funduq, p. 91. The latter adds that he was a Zoroastrian born in Adharbāyjān, who wrote several works on logic and music, but that he was not skilled in Arabic theology (*al-kalām al-ᶜarabī.*) He died in 458/ 1066, "thirty years after the death of Abū ᶜAlī." Ibn Funduq, *ibid.*

12. "Abū al-Rayḥān al-Bīrūnī": Ibn Sīnā's contemporary and chief rival as the greatest philosopher-scientist of that time. Born in Khwārazm in 362/973, he was a client at many of the same courts as Ibn Sīnā: the Sāmānids, the Khwārazm-shāhs, the Ziyārids in Jurjān, and the Būyids in al-Rayy. They may have come into personal contact in one or more of these courts, although neither man mentions it. Their correspondence is mentioned by al-Bīrūnī in *al-Athār al-bāqiya ᶜan al-qurūn al-khāliya* ed. C. Eduard Sachau (Leipzig, 1923; rpt. Baghdād, n.d.), p. 257; tr. Sachau, *The Chronology of Ancient Nations* (London, 1879), p. 247. According to Ibn Funduq, p. 95, the correspondence became bitter, especially when al-Bīrūnī questioned some of Ibn Sīnā's replies. Ibn Sīnā allowed his best pupil, al-Maᶜṣūmī, to read al-Bīrūnī's objections in a mocking manner and write an insulting answer to al-Bīrūnī. See Ibn Funduq, pp. 29 and 62, for further information on these disputes. Also see D. J. Boilot, "al-Bīrūnī," *EI*², I, 1236-38.

13. "the prince Abū Bakr Muḥammad ibn ᶜUbayd": Although all of the MSS of the autobiography / biography read "the prince" (*al-amīr*), MSS of the work itself read "to the faithful shaykh" (*li'l-shaykh al-amīn*). He is called either Abū Bakr Muḥammad or Abū Bakr ibn Muḥammad. See Mahdavi, p. 39. However, Ibn Funduq, p. 33, says that Ibn Sīnā dedicated this work to "the faithful wazīr (*al-shaykh al-wazīr al-amīn*) Abū Saᶜd al-Hamadhānī."

14. "Abū ᶜAlī al-Naysābūrī": The biographical dictionaries do not list this name.

15. "*Questions of Ḥunayn*": Ḥunayn ibn Isḥāq (d. 260 / [873], according to al-Qifṭī, p. 173, and *Fihrist*, p. 294; or 264 / [877], according to Ibn Uṣaybiᶜa, I, 190), the Nestorian translator of Greek scientific and philosophical works. He also wrote a number of treatises on medicine, of which his *Questions* is called an introduction (*madkhal*) to medicine by Ibn Abī Uṣaybiᶜa, I, 197.

16. "Abū Saᶜīd ibn Abī al-Khayr": One of the most famous Ṣūfis of Ibn Sīnā's time (he was born in 357/967 and died in 440/1049), he and Ibn Sīnā probably never met, despite the many accounts to the contrary. See H. Ritter, "Abū Saᶜīd

Faḍl Allāh ibn Abī'l-Khayr," *EI*², I, 147; but cf. R.A. Nicholson, *Studies in Islamic Mysticism* (Cambridge, 1921; rpt. 1967), p. 42. They were also reported to have carried on a correspondence, and Mahdavi, pp. 3-11, lists ten works by Ibn Sīnā written in response to questions by Abū Saᶜid ibn Abī al-Khayr.

17. "Abū al-Faraj, the Hamadhānī doctor": This person may be Abū al-Faraj ibn Abī Saᶜīd al-Yamāmī, who met Ibn Sīnā and corresponded with him. See Ibn Abī Uṣaybiᶜa, I, 239. According to Ibn Abī Uṣaybiᶜa, Abū al-Faraj would have studied with both his father, Abū Saᶜīd, and Ibn Sīnā.

18. "*the Angle . . . has no Magnitude*": Mahdavi, p. 122 states that this work is identical with item No. 22 in this bibliography.

19. "the logic of the *Essential Philosophy*": Three of the other MSS—A, J, and N—state parenthetically that the *Small Epitome* on logic became the logic of the *Najāt*, not that of the *Essential Philosophy*. See above, item No. 29.

20. "*Main Questions*": This title probably refers to the work of the same name by al-Fārābī. See R. Walzer, "al-Fārābī," *EI*², II, 780, for this title.

21. "Abū al-Ḥasan . . . al-Sahlī": See Notes to the Translation of the Biography, n. 41.

22. "Abū al-Ḥasan al-ᶜĀmirī": Muḥammad ibn Yūsuf (d. 382/992), a philosopher in the tradition of al-Kindī (d. *ca.* 259/873), he wrote a history of Greek philosophy which was mentioned as being extant in Bukhārā in 375/985. See F. E. Peters, *Aristotle and the Arabs*, New York University Studies in Near Eastern Civilization, No. 1 (New York, 1968), pp. 159, 256.

23. "the *Position . . . Heavens*": This work is probably the same as item No. 44 in this bibliography.

24. "*Substance and Accident*": This work is probably the same as item No. 88 in this bibliography.

25. "refuting . . . Ibn al-Ṭayyib": This work is probably the same as item No. 26 in this bibliography.

26. "Abū ᶜAbd Allāh, the lawyer": His favorite pupil, Abū ᶜAbd Allāh Aḥmad (or possibly Muḥammad ibn Aḥmad) al-Maᶜṣūmī. Ibn Sīnā compared al-Maᶜṣūmī's relationship to himself as that of Aristotle to Plato. See Ibn Funduq, pp. 95-96; *GAL*, I, 458, and *GAL, S*, I, 828.

27. "*Sorrow and its Causes*": This work is probably the same as item No. 80 in this bibliography.

28. "An essay . . . *Confusion*": This work is probably the same as item No. 54 in this bibliography. Although the name of the person for whom it was written is not identical with the name of the person for whom the work on alchemy was written: Abū ᶜAbd Allāh al-Ḥūsayn ibn Sahl ibn Muḥammad al-Sahlī, rather than Abū al-Ḥusayn Aḥmad ibn Muḥammad al-Sahli, the title of the work is similar to one of the subtitles of item No. 54 given by one the MSS (B): A Hidden Matter.

APPENDIX I

SHORTER BIBLIOGRAPHY OF IBN SINA'S WORKS

TITLE	NUMERICAL ORDER IN Q	IAU	Ibn Funduq	Longer bibliography
1. The Compilation	1	1	5	6
2. The Sum and Substance	2	2	6	3
3. Good Works and Evil	3	4	7	4
4. The Shifāʾ	4	5	8	2
5. The Qānūn	5	6	9	7
6. Comprehensive Observations	6	7	3	10
7. The Judgment	7	3	10	5
8. The Najāt	8	8	11	14
9. Guidance	9	9	12	16
10. Instructions[1]	10	..	13	15
11. The Middle Summary	11	..	1	8
12. The ʿAlāʾī	12	..	14	13
13. The Colic	13	10	..	17
14. The Arabic Language	14	11	15	12
15. Cardiac Remedies	15	12	16	19
16. The Epitome[2]	16	13	17	29
17. The Eastern Philosophy	17	14	..	45
18. Explanation of Modals[3]	18	15	19	28
19. The Return	19	16	21	11
20. The Origin and the Return	20	17	2 & 20	9
21. Conversations	21	18	..	41
22. Foreordination and Destiny	22	19	23	33
23. Astronomical Instruments	23	20	25	53
24. The Object of the "Categories".	24	21	26	55
25. Logic	25	22	27	30

[1]Longer bibliography: Instructions and Remarks.
[2]Longer bibliography: The Large Epitome.
[3]Longer bibliography: Conversions of Modals.

Title	Numerical Order in: Q	IAU	Ibn Funduq	Longer bibliography
26. Poems on Majesty and Philosophy[4]	26	23	..	68
27. The Consonants[5]	27	24	29	21
28. Consideration of Dialectical Topics	28	25	30	46
29. Summary of Euclid	29	26	31	66
30. Summary on the Pulse	30	27	32	20
31. Definitions	31	28	33	25
32. Celestial Bodies[6]	32	29	24	49
33. Instruction in the Science of Logic	33	30	..	35
34. The Branches of Philosophy[7]	34	31	34	36
35. Limit and Infinity[8]	35	32	35	38
36. Testament	36	33	..	60
37. Ḥayy ibn Yaqẓān	37	34	36	18
38. The Dimensions of a Body are not part of its Essence	38	35	37	..
39. Endive	39	36	38	34
40. The Impossibility of the same thing being a Substance and an Accident	40	37	..	88
41. Knowledge of Zayd is not the Knowledge of ᶜAmr	41	38	..	61
42. Letters to Friends and Officials[9]	42	39	..	69, 72
43. Letters about Questions which passed between him and other learned men[10]	43	40	39	89
44. Comments on the Qānūn	44	41	..	..
45. Essential Philosophy	45	42	..	27
46. The Net and the Bird[11]	46	43	..	24
47. Summary of the "Almagest" (*mukhtaṣar al-majisṭī*)	..	..	4	..

[4]Longer bibliography: Odes and Poems.
[5]Longer bibliography: Phonetics.
[6]Ibn Funduq: *al-ᶜulwiyya* in place of *al-samāwiyya.*
[7]Ibn Funduq: *ᶜulūm al-ḥikma* in place of *al-ḥikma.*
[8]Longer bibliography: Infinity.
[9]Longer bibliography: Treatises, etc.; and Twenty Questions.
[10]Ibn Funduq: ... between him and learned men of the age.
[11]Longer bibliography: The Bird.

Title	Numerical Order in			
	Q	IAU	Ibn Funduq	Longer bibliography
48. Sacred Philosophy (*al-ḥikmat al-qudsiyya*)	..	..	18	..
49. Necessities (*al-muqtaḍayāt*)	..	..	22	..
50. The Gift (*al-tuḥfa*)	..	..	28	..

APPENDIX II

Longer Bibliography of Ibn Sina's Works

Title	Numerical Order in							
	A	B	J	N	IAU	Ibn Funduq	Mahdavi	Anawati
1. The Supplements	1	2	1	1	1	5	..	..
2. The Shifāʾ	2	1	2	2	2	3	84	14
3. The Sum and Substance	3	3	3	3	3	4	..	..
4. Good Works and Evil	4	4	4	4	4	84	40	249
5. The Judgment[1]	5	5	5	5	5	7	35	6
6. The Compilation	6	6	6	6	6	1	62	10
7. The Qānūn	7	7	7	7	7	6	98	140
8. The Middle [Summary]	8	8	8	8	8	16	108	45
9. The Origin and the Return	9	9	9	9	9	19	106	195
10. Comprehensive Observations	10	10	10	10	10	..	..	..
11. The Return	11	11	11	11	11	37	121	74, 77 109, 199 201
12. The Arabic Language	12	13	12	12	12	105	104	..
13. The ʿAlāʾī Philosophy[2]	13	12 14	13	13	13	40	72	11, 13
14. The Najāt	14	15	14	14	14	8	118	23
15. The Instructions and Remarks[3]	15	95	15	15	15	11	27	3, 239
16. Guidance	16	16	16	16	16	50	130	24
17. The Colic	17	17	17	17	17	77	101	142

[1]The Judgment and Equity (*al-inṣāf wa'l-intiṣāf*).
[2]The ʿAlāʾī.
[3]The Instructions (*al-ishārāt*).

Title	Numerical Order in							
	A	B	J	N	IAU	Ibn Funduq	Mahdavi	Anawati
18. Ḥayy ibn Yaqẓān	18	19	18	18	18	53	65	219
19. Cardiac Drugs	19	20	19	19	19	41	14	111
20. The Pulse	20	21	20	20	20	83	117	149
21. Phonetics	21	22	21	21	21	..	25	47
22. The Angle	22	23	22	22	22	57	80	160
23. Natural Faculties	23	24	23	23	23	..	76	141
24. The Bird[4]	24	25	24	24	24	32	88	229
25. Definitions	25	26	25	25	25	43	57	9
26. Refuting Ibn al-Ṭayyib[5]	26	27	26	26	26 98	80	76	141
27. Essential Philosophy	27	28	27	27	27	12	93	15
28. Conversions of Modals[6]	28	29	28	28	28	18	42	..
29. The Large Epitome	29	30	29	29	30	23	114	44
30. The Ode[7]	30	31	30	30	31	64	22	25, 33
31. Discourse on Unity	31	33	31	31	29	..	70	177, 194
32. The Attainment of Happiness	32	34	32	32	32	..	43	84
33. Foreordination and Destiny	33	35	33	33	33	114	100	193
34. Endive	34	36	34	34	34	44	131	150, 272
35. Instruction in the Science of Logic	35	37	35	35	35	15	28	37
36. The Branches of Philosophy and the Sciences[8]	36	38	36	36	36	55 56	32	4
37. Oxymel	37	39	37	37	37	112	81	132
38. Infinity[9]	38	40	38	38	38	30	64	75

[4]The Treatise called the Bird (*al-risālat al-mawsūma bi'l-ṭayr*).

[5]A Treatise Refuting an Essay of Abū al-Faraj (*risāla fī al-radd ʿalā maqāla li-Abī al-Faraj*).

[6]Explanation of Modals (*bayān dhawāt al-jiha*).

[7]Poem on Logic (*urjūza fī al-manṭiq*).

[8]The Branches of the Sciences (*aqsān al-ʿulūm*); and The Branches of Philosophy (*aqsām al-ḥikma*).

[9]On Finiteness and Infinity (*fī al-tanāhī wa'l-lā tanāhī*).

Title	Numerical Order in							
	A	B	J	N	IAU	Ibn Funduq	Mahdavi	Anawati
39. Commentaries[10]	39	41	39	39	39	88	4w	260, 266 268
40. Characteristics of the Equator	40	42	40	40	40	..	..	..
41. Discussions	41	43	41	41	41	10	105	19, 257
42. Ten Questions[11]	..	44	42	42	42	60	6, 7	2, 38
43. Sixteen Questions[12]	43	45	43	43	43	59	5	1, 54
44. The Position of the Earth[13]	44	46	44	44	44 94	29	91	168
45. The Eastern Philosophy	45	47	45	45	45	13	63	12, 41
46. Consideration of Dialectical Topics	46	48	46	46	46	20	48	26
47. The Error in saying that Quantity belongs to Substance	47	49	47	47	..	..	67	68
48. Introduction to the Art of Music[14]	48	50	48	48	47	70	232	165
49. The Celestial Bodies[15]	49	51	49	49	48	51	53	53
50. Correcting Errors in Medical Treatment[16]	50	52	50	50	49	42	75	130
51. The Nature of Observation	51	53	51	51	51	..	..	..
52. Ethics	52	54	52	52	52	54	13	246

[10]Commentaries on Logic (*taʿālīq fī al-manṭiq*).

[11]Answers to Ten Questions (*ajwibat ʿashr masāʾil*).

[12]Answers to Abū al-Rayḥān al-Bīrūnī which he sent to him from Khwārazm (*ajwibat Abī al-Rayḥān al-Bīrūnī anfadhahā ilayhi min Khwārazm*).

[13]On the Cause of the Earth's Remaining in its Position (*fī ʿillat qiyām al-arḍ fī ḥayyizihi*).

[14]Treatise on Music other than [the one in] the Shifāʾ (*risāla fī al-mūsīqā siwā al-shifāʾ*).

[15]On the Knowledge of the Celestial Bodies (*fī maʿrifat al-ajrām al-samāwiyya*).

[16]Correcting some types of Error (*tadāruk anwāʿ al-khaṭaʾ*).

Title	Numerical Order in A	B	J	N	IAU	Ibn Funduq	Mahdavi	Anawati
53. Astronomical Instruments	53	55	53	53	54	..	1	164
54. Alchemy[17]	54	56	54	54	53 102	72	33	154
55. The Object of the "Categories"	55	57	55	55	55	..	..	..
56. The Aḍḥawiyya letter	56	58	56	56	56	73	30	200
57. The Defense of Poets	57	59	57	57	57	..	184	30
58. The Definition of Body	58	60	58	58	58	..	56	56, 60 64, 72
59. Throne Philosophy	59	61	59	59	59	118	61	179, 183
60. Testament	60	62	60	60	60	52	92	82, 232
61. The Knowledge of Zayd is not the Knowledge of ᶜAmr	61	63	61	61	61	34	..	..
62. The Management of Troops[18]	62	64	62	62	62	103	46	252
63. Disputes with Abū ᶜAlī al-Naysābūrī	63	65	63	63	63	..	..	..
64. Discourses, etc.	64	66	64	64	64	..	69, 70 71	220, 188 194, 129
65. A Reply containing an Apology[19]	65	67	65	65	65	74	34	204, 257
66. Summary of Euclid	66	68	66	67	66	..	219	169
67. Arithmetic	67	69	67	68	67	..	221	170
68. Odes and Poems	68	70	68	69	68	90	29	50
69. Treatises, etc.	69	71	69	66	69	86	..	..
70. Commentaries on the Questions of Ḥunayn	70	72	70	70	70	110	110	144
71. Medical Principles and Practice[20]	71	73	71	71	71	106	73	128

[17]On a Hidden Matter (*fī amr mastūr*).

[18]The Management of the Household (*tadbīr al-manzil*).

[19]A Letter to Abū ᶜUbayd al-Jūzjānī Refuting the Charge that he Contradicted the Qurᵓān (*risāla ilā Abī ᶜUbayd al-Jūzjānī fī al-intifāᵓ ᶜammā nusiba ilayhi min muᶜāradat al-Qurᵓān*).

[20]Medical Rules (*dustūr ṭibbī*).

Title	Numerical Order in A	B	J	N	IAU	Ibn Funduq	Mahdavi	Anawati
72. Twenty Questions[21]	72	74	72	72	73	61	..	..
73. Medical Questions[22]	73	75	73	73	72	78	..	..
74. Questions called Rarities	74	76	74	74	..	..	..	..
75. Questions explained in Notes	75	77	75	75	74	..	..	..
76. Answers to Simple Questions	76	78	76	76	75	..	..	..
77. Letter to the *ᶜulamā*ᵓ of Baghdād	77	80	77	77	76	..	78	..
78. Letter to a Friend	78	81	78	78	77	..	..	..
79. Answers to a Number of Questions	79	82	79	79	78	..	..	..
80. Explaining the Essence of Sorrow[23]	80	83	80	80	79 101	108	59	217
81. Commentary on Aristotle's *De Anima*	81	84	81	81	80	..	177	87
82. The Soul[24]	82	85	82	82	81	97 98 99	120	102
83. The Refutation of Astrology	83	86	83	83	82	..	2	52
84. Anecdotes on Grammar	84	87	84	84	83	..	..	..
85. Metaphysical Chapters[25]	85	88	85	85	84	81	195 133	187, 206 175
86. Chapters on the Soul and on Physics	86	89	86	86	85	..	..	..
87. Letter to Abū Saᶜīd ibn Abī al-Khayr	87	90	87	87	86	62	4z	225, 256

[21] Answers to Another Twenty Questions (*ajwibat ᶜishrīn masāᵓil ukhrā*).
[22] Medical Decisions Brought Out in his Sessions (*fuṣūl ṭibbiyya jarat fī majlisihi*).
[23] On the Nature of Sorrow (*fī māhiyyat al-ḥuzn*).
[24] Treatise on the Soul (*risāla fī al-nafs*)—three identical titles.
[25] Treatise Proving the First Principle (*risāla fī ithbāt al-mabdaᵓ al-awwal*).

Title	Numerical Order in							
	A	B	J	N	IAU	Ibn Funduq	Mahdavi	Anawati
88. The Impossibility of the same thing being a Substance and an Accident	88	91	88	88	87 96	36	68	59
89. Questions which passed between him and other learned men[26]	89	92	89	89	88	75	4–11	35, *et al.*
90. Comments[27]	90	93	90	90	89	9	205	94
91. The Traveled and Uninhabited Parts of the Earth	91	94	91	91	90	..	..	..
92. The Angle formed by the Circumference and the Tangent has no Magnitude	92	18	92	92	91	..	80	160
93. The Small Epitome on Logic	..	32	..	..	93	26	115	43
94. Main Questions	..	79	..	..	..	..	..	..
95. Seven Essays for al-Suhaylī	..	..	..	..	50	..	..	..
96. Answers to Questions posed by al-ᶜĀmirī	..	..	..	..	92	..	..	..
97. Keys to the Treasures, in Logic	..	..	..	..	95	..	..	..
98. The Interpretation of Dreams	..	..	..	..	97	..	47	101, 156
99. On Love	..	..	..	..	99	45	90	230
100. On Human Faculties	..	..	..	..	100	35	206	95

[26]Anawati lists twenty-two works which would fit under this title.
[27]Comments (*al-taᶜlīqāt*), without any further designation.

APPENDIX III

Chronological Order of Ibn Sina's Works

It is difficult to place Ibn Sīnā's works in chronological order for several reasons. First, there is the question of checking the authenticity of the works attributed to Ibn Sīnā in the medieval and modern bibliographies. This would include determining how many works have been given two or more titles, hence consolidating the number of works and reducing the total to a corpus of genuine works by Ibn Sīnā (probably somewhere between one hundred and two hundred titles.)

The next obstacle arises when one considers the nature of many of his works. Most of his writings are summaries, compendia, and epitomes of his larger works. According to the earliest bibliographies, he included some of these summaries as sections of larger works. Until one can do a detailed study of Ibn Sīnā's stylistic development based on the works that can be dated exactly, it will be impossible to tell if a particular treatise on the soul, for example, is an early or a later summary of his knowledge of the subject.

Another problem is related to his intellectual development and mental growth. He himself claimed that he added nothing to his store of knowledge after his eighteenth year, and while this is certainly an exaggeration—al-Jūzjānī reports that he later studied philology for three years in Iṣfahān—he does seem to have achieved his mastery of most of the topics of philosophy and medicine at this early age. It is therefore difficult to see how a study of particular topics discussed by Ibn Sīnā can provide any clues as to the relative date of the composition of a given work.

We are left then with three sources of information to be used in dating Ibn Sīnā's works. The first is Ibn Sīnā's own—or al-Jūzjānī's—notice of a particular work in the autobiography/biography. This allows us to date with some certainty several of the major works, such as the *Shifā*ᵓ, the *Qānūn*, and the *Najāt*. The second source is the author of the longer bibliography which was appended to most of the early manuscripts of the autobiography/biography. This anonymous compiler included in some of his notices the name of the recipient of the particular work, thus providing enough information to date several additional works not specifically mentioned by Ibn Sīnā or al-Jūzjānī.

The third source, and the one with the greatest potential for determining the exact dating, is the specific manuscript itself. A number of manuscripts contain dedications as part of their opening remarks. Some manuscripts contain references to biographical data, or refer to previous works of Ibn Sīnā, so they can be dated more or less precisely. However, this source can only be exhausted when all of the manuscripts have been authenticated and examined closely for such references. I have been able to make this kind of examination only superficially, using the descriptions of the manuscripts in Mahdavi's and Anawati's bibliographies. The following chronological list is based on this examination, as well as the information provided by Ibn Sīnā, al-Jūzjānī, and the compiler of the long bibliography.

Works written in Bukhārā (i.e., sometime before 392/1002) were the **Sum and Substance* (number 3 in the long bibliography), *Good Works and Evil* (4), the *Compilation* (6), +Ten Questions (42), +*Sixteen Questions* (43), the +*Defense of Poets* (57), and the *Soul*, known as the *Chapters* (82).

Works written in Gurgānj (392/1002–402/1012) were the *Ode* on logic (30), the *Position of the Earth* (44), *Correcting Errors in Medical Treatment* (50), and *Alchemy* (54), all of which were dedicated to al-Suhaylī (al-Sahlī in the manuscripts.)

Works written in Jurjān (402/1012–405/1014) were the *Middle Summary* (8), the *Origin and the Return* (9), **Comprehensive Observations* (10), the *Angle* (22), and Book I of the *Qānūn* (7).

Works written in al-Rayy (405/1014–15) were the *Return* (11), and a portion of the *Qānūn*.

Works written in Hamadhān (405/1015–415/1024) were *Cardiac Drugs* (19), *Guidance* (16), the *Colic* (17), *Ḥayy ibn Yaqẓān* (18), a letter to the *ʿulamāʾ* of Baghdād (77),* a letter to a friend (78), the final parts of the *Qānūn*, and several parts of the *Shifāʾ* (2): the "Physics" (except the sections on Animals and Plants), the "Metaphysics," and one section of the "Logic."

The largest number of works which can be dated were written in Iṣfahān (415/1024–428/1037). These works include the + *Supplements* (1), the + *Judgement* (5), the +*Arabic Language* (12), the *ʿAlāʾī Philosophy* (13), the *Najāt* (14), the *Instructions and Remarks* (15), the *Pulse* (20), *Phonetics* (21), *Foreordination and Destiny* (33), *Discussions* with Bahmanyār (41), *Eastern Philosophy* (45), *Astronomical Instruments* (53), *Throne Philosophy* (59), commentary on Aristotle's *De Anima* (81), the *Aḍḥawiyya Letter on the Return* (56), and the final parts of the *Shifāʾ*.

The remainder of the works listed in the medieval bibliographies cannot be precisely dated at this time, for the reasons given above.

---

*This work is not known to have survived to this time.

+This title is found in both the medieval and modern bibliographies, but the works so designated may not be identical.

BIBLIOGRAPHY

Afnan, Soheil M. *Avicenna: His Life and Works.* London, 1958.

Aḥmad, S. Maqbūl. "Djughrāfiyā." *Encyclopaedia of Islam.* 2nd ed. Vol. II.

al-Ahwānī, Aḥmad Fuʾād, ed. *Nukat fī aḥwāl al-Shaykh al-Raʾīs Ibn Sīnā.* Dhikrā Ibn Sīnā, Vol. III. Cairo, 1952.

Anawati, Georges C., O.P. *Muʾallafāt Ibn Sīnā.* Cairo, 1950.

Arberry, Arthur J. *Aspects of Islamic Civilization.* London, 1964; rpt. Ann Arbor, 1967.

———. *Avicenna on Theology.* The Wisdom of the East Series. London, 1951.

Arnaldez, Roger. "Falsafa." *Encyclopaedia of Islam.* 2nd ed. Vol. II.

ᶜAufī, Muḥammad. *Lubāb al-albāb.* Ed. E.G. Browne and M. Qazwīnī. 2 vols. London and Leiden, 1903-1906.

Barthold, W. *Turkestan down to the Mongol Invasion.* 3rd ed. Gibb Memorial Series, New Series, Vol. V. London, 1968.

———, and Frye, Richard N. "Bukhārā." *Encyclopaedia of Islam.* 2nd ed. Vol I.

Bayhaqī, Abū al-Faḍl Muḥammad ibn Ḥusayn. *Tārīkh-i Masᶜūdī.* Ed. Qāsim Ghānī and ᶜAbbās A. Fayyāḍ. Teheran, 1324/1945.

Bergh, Simon van den. "Djins." *Encyclopaedia of Islam.* 2nd ed. Vol. II.

al-Bīrūnī, Abū al-Rayḥān Muḥammad ibn Aḥmad. *Kitāb al-tafhīm li-awāʾil ṣināᶜat al-tanjīm.* Ed. and trans. R. Ramsay Wright. London, 1934.

———. *al-Athār al-bāqiya ᶜan al-qurūn al-khāliya.* Ed. C. Eduard Sachau. Leipzig, 1923; rpt. Baghdad, n.d. Trans. Sachau as *The Chronology of Ancient Nations.* London, 1879.

Blachère, Régis. "al-Azharī." *Encyclopaedia of Islam.* 2nd ed. Vol. I.

Bosworth, Clifford E. "Dailamis in Central Iran: the Kākūyids of Jibāl and Yazd". *Iran,* VIII (1970), 73–95.

———. *The Ghaznavids: Their Empire in Afghanistan and Eastern Iran, 999–1040.* Edinburgh, 1963.

———. *The Islamic Dynasties.* Islamic Surveys, Vol. V. Edinburgh, 1967.

———. "The Political and Dynastic History of the Iranian World (A.D. 1000–1217)." *The Cambridge History of Iran.* Vol. V: *The Saljuq and Mongol Periods.* Ed. J.A. Boyle. Cambridge, 1968.

Brand, Charles M., ed. *Icon and Minaret.* Englewood Cliffs, N.J., 1969.

Brockelmann, Carl. *Geschichte der arabischen Literatur.* 2nd ed. 2 vols. and 3 supplementary vols. Leiden, 1937–1949.

Browne, Edward G. *A Literary History of Persia.* 4 vols. Cambridge, 1902–1924; rpt. Cambridge, 1956.

Cahen, Claude. "Ḍay^{c}a." *Encyclopaedia of Islam.* 2nd ed. Vol. II.

———. "Ibn al-^{c}Amīd." *Encyclopaedia of Islam.* 2nd ed. Vol. III.

———, and Pellat, Charles. "Ibn ^{c}Abbād." *Encyclopaedia of Islam.* 2nd ed. Vol. III.

Canard, Marius. "Da^{c}wa." *Encyclopaedia of Islam.* 2nd ed. Vol. II.

Casanova, Paul. "Les Ispehbeds de Firim." *A Volume of Oriental Studies Presented to Professor Edward G. Browne.* Cambridge, 1922.

Dozy, Reinhart P.A. *Supplément aux dictionnaires arabes.* Leiden, 1881; rpt. Beirut, 1968.

Dunlop, Derrick M. "Bīmāristān." *Encyclopaedia of Islam.* 2nd ed. Vol. I.

al-Fārābī, Abū Naṣr Muḥammad ibn Muḥammad ibn Ṭarkhān. "Fī aghrāḍ kitāb 'Mā ba^{c}da al-ṭabī^{c}a.' " *Alfarabi's philosophische Abhandlungen.* Ed. Friedrich H. Dieterici. Leiden, 1890.

Frye, Richard N. "Balkh." *Encyclopaedia of Islam.* 2nd ed. Vol. I.

Gabrieli, Francesco. "Adab." *Encyclopaedia of Islam.* 2nd ed. Vol. I.

Gardīzī, Abū Sa^{c}īd ^{c}Abd al-Ḥayy ibn al-Daḥḥāk. *Ẓayn al-akhbār.* Ed. ^{c}Abd al-Ḥayy Ḥabībī. Teheran, 1347/[1969].

Goichon, Amélie-Marie. *Lexique de la langue philosophique d'Ibn Sina.* Paris, 1938.

Goldziher, Ignaz, and Schacht, Joseph. "Fiḳh." *Encyclopaedia of Islam.* 2nd ed. Vol. II.

Ḥamd Allāh Mustawfī al-Qazwīnī. *Nuzhat al-qulūb.* Ed. and trans. G. Le Strange. Gibb Memorial Series, Vol. XXIII. 2 vols. London and Leiden, 1913–1915.

Haywood, John A. *Arabic Lexicography.* 2nd ed. Leiden, 1965.

Hitti, Philip K. *Makers of Arab History.* New York, 1968.

Hodgson, Marshall G.S. "Bāṭiniyya." *Encyclopaedia of Islam.* 2nd ed. Vol. I.

Huart, Clement I. *Les calligraphes et miniaturistes de l'Orient musulman.* Paris, 1908.

———. "Kāghad." *Encyclopaedia of Islam.* 1st ed. Vol. II.

Ḥudūd al-^{c}ālam. Trans. Vladimir Minorsky. 2nd ed. Ed. C. E. Bosworth. Gibb Memorial Series, Vol. XI. London, 1970.

Ibn Abī Uṣaybi^{c}a, Abū al-^{c}Abbās Aḥmad ibn al-Qāsim. *^{c}Uyūn al-anbā$^{\supset}$ fī ṭabaqāt al-aṭibbā$^{\supset}$.* Ed. August Muller. 3 vols. Kőnigsberg and Cairo, 1882-1884.

Ibn al-Athīr, Abū al-Ḥasan ^{c}Alī ibn Abī al-Karam Athīr al-Dīn Muḥammad. *al-Kāmil fī al-ta$^{\supset}$rīkh.* Ed. Carl J. Tornberg. 14 vols. Leiden, 1851–1876; rpt. Beirut, 1966.

Ibn Funduq, Ẓahīr al-Dīn Abū al-Ḥasan ^{c}Alī ibn Zayd al-Bayhaqī. *Tatimmat Ṣiwān al-ḥikma.* Ed. Muḥammad Shafī^{c}. 2 vols. Lahore, 1935.

———. *Durrat al-akhbār.* Ed. Muḥammad Shafī^{c} as Vol. II of the *Tatimmat Ṣiwān al-ḥikma.* Lahore, 1935.

Ibn Ḥawqal, Abū al-Qāsim. *Ṣūrat al-arḍ.* Ed. Michael J. de Goeje. *Bibliotheca Geographorum Arabicorum,* Vol. II. Leiden, 1873.

Ibn al-ᶜImād, ᶜAbd al-Ḥayy. *Shadharāt al-dhahab fī akhbār man dhahab.* 8 vols. Beirut, 1965.

Ibn Khaldūn, ᶜAbd al-Raḥmān ibn Muḥammad. *al-Muqaddima.* Cairo, n.d.

———. *The Muqaddimah.* Trans. Franz Rosenthal. Bollingen Series, Vol. XLIII. 3 vols. New York, 1958.

Ibn Khallikān, Aḥmad ibn Muḥammad. *Wafayāt al-aᶜyān.* Trans. W. McG. de Slane. 4 vols. Paris, 1842–1871.

Ibn al-Nadīm, Abū al-Faraj Muḥammad ibn Abī Yaᶜqūb Isḥāq. *al-Fihrist.* Ed. Gustave Flügel. 2 vols. Leipzig, 1871–1872; rpt. Beirut, 1964.

Ibn Sīnā, Abū ᶜAlī al-Ḥusayn ibn ᶜAbd Allāh. *Kitāb al-majmūᶜ.* Ed. Dr. Muḥammad S. Sālim. Cairo, 1969.

Justi, Ferdinand. *Iranisches Namenbuch.* Marburg, 1895.

Khwāndamīr, Ghiyāth al-Dīn Muḥammad. *Tārīkh al-wuzarāᵓ.* MS. Cleveland Public Library. John G. White Collection.

al-Khwārazmī, Abū ᶜAbd Allāh Muḥammad ibn Aḥmad ibn Yūsuf. *Kitāb mafātīḥ al-ᶜulūm.* Ed. G. van Vloten. Leiden, 1895; rpt. Leiden, 1968.

Krenkow, Fritz. "al-Ṣābī." *Encyclopaedia of Islam.* 1st ed. Vol. IV.

Lane, Edward W. *Arabic-English Lexicon.* 8 parts. London, 1863–1893; rpt. New York, 1956.

Le Strange, Guy. *The Lands of the Eastern Caliphate.* Cambridge, 1905; rpt. New York, 1966.

Levey, Martin, and al-Khaledy, Noory. *The Medical Formulary of al-Samarqandī.* Philadelphia, 1967.

Maas, Paul. *Textual Criticism.* Trans. from the 3rd German ed. by Barbara Flower. Oxford, 1958.

Mahdavī, Yaḥyā. *Fihrist-i muṣannafāt-i Ibn-i Sīnā.* Publications of the University of Teheran, No. 206. Teheran, 1333/1954.

Marᶜashī, Ẓahīr al-Dīn. *Tārīkh-i Ṭabaristān wa Rūyān wa Māzandarān.* Ed. Muḥammad H. Tasbīḥī. Teheran, 1345/1966.

Miles, George C. "Dirham." *Encyclopaedia of Islam.* 2nd ed. Vol. II.

Minorsky, Vladimir. "ᶜAnnāzids." *Encyclopaedia of Islam.* 2nd ed. Vol. I.

Mīrkhwānd, Muḥammad ibn Khāwand-Shāh ibn Maḥmūd. *Histoire des Samanides.* Ed. and trans. Charles Defrémery. Paris, 1845.

Miskawayh, Abū ᶜAbd Allāh Aḥmad ibn Muḥammad ibn Yaᶜqūb. *Tajārib al-umam.* Ed. and trans. Henry F. Amedroz and David S. Margoliouth, with the continuations of Abū Shujāᶜ al-Rūdhrāwarī and Hilāl ibn al-Muḥassin, as *The Eclipse of the ᶜAbbāsid Caliphate.* 6 vols. London, 1920-1921.

Nafīsī, Saᶜīd. *Sar-gudhasht-i Ibn-i Sīnā.* Teheran, 1331/ [1952].

Naṣr, Seyyed Hossein. *Three Muslim Sages.* Cambridge, Mass., 1964.

———. *Introduction to Islamic Cosmological Doctrines.* Cambridge, Mass., 1964.

Nicholson, Reynold A., *Studies in Islamic Mysticism.* Cambridge, 1921; rpt. Cambridge, 1967.

Niẓām al-Mulk. *Siyar al-mulūk*, or *Siyāsat-nāmah*. Ed. Hubert Darke. Teheran, 1340/1962.

———. *The Book of Government or Rules for Kings*. Trans. Hubert Darke. London, 1960.

Niẓāmī ᶜArūḍī, Aḥmad ibn ᶜUmar ibn ᶜAlī al-Samarqandī. *Chahār maqālah*. Ed. Mīrzā Muḥammad Qazwīnī. Gibb Memorial Series, Vol. XI, part 1. Leiden and London, 1910.

———. *Chahār maqālah*. Trans. E.G. Browne. London, 1900.

O'Leary, De Lacy. *How Greek Science Passed to the Arabs*. London, 1949.

Pellat, Charles. "Ḥisāb al-ᶜAḳd." *Encyclopaedia of Islam*. 2nd ed. Vol. III.

Peters, Francis E. *Aristotle and the Arabs*. New York University Studies in Near Eastern Civilization, No. 1. New York, 1968.

al-Qifṭī, Abū al-Ḥasan ᶜAlī ibn Yūsuf. *Taʾrīkh al-ḥukamāʾ*. Ed. Julius Lippert. Leipzig, 1903.

Ritter, Helmut. "Abū Saᶜīd Faḍl Allāh ibn Abī al-Khayr." *Encyclopaedia of Islam*. 2nd ed. Vol. I.

Rypka, Jan. *History of Iranian Literature*. Dordrecht-Holland, 1968.

al-Samᶜānī, ᶜAbd al-Karīm ibn Muḥammad. *Kitāb al-ansāb*. Ed. in facsimile by D.S. Margoliouth. Gibb Memorial Series, Vol. XX. London and Leiden, 1912.

Sayili, Aydin. *The Observatory in Islam*. Publications of the Turkish Historical Society, Series VII, No. 38. Ankara, 1960.

Steingass, Francis J. *Persian-English Dictionary*. London, 1892.

Stern, Samuel M. "The Early Ismāᶜīlī Missionaries in North-West Persia and in Khurāsān and Transoxania." *Bulletin of the School of Oriental and African Studies*, XXIII (1960), 56–90.

al-Thaᶜālibī, Abū Manṣūr ᶜAbd al-Malik ibn Muḥammad. *Tatimmat al-Yatīma*. Ed. ᶜAbbās Iqbāl. 2 vols. Teheran, 1353/1934.

———. *Yatīmat al-dahr*. Ed. Muḥammad M. ᶜAbd al-Ḥamīd. 2nd ed. 4 vols. Cairo, 1375/1956.

Walzer, Richard. *Greek into Arabic*. Oriental Studies, Vol. I. Oxford, 1962.

———. "al-Fārābī." *Encyclopaedia of Islam*. 2nd ed. Vol. II.

Wickens, G.M., ed. *Avicenna: Scientist and Philosopher*. London, 1952.

Yāqūt, Shihāb al-Dīn Abū ᶜAbd Allāh Yaᶜqūb ibn ᶜAbd Allāh al-Ḥamawī. *Irshād al-arīb*. Ed. D.S. Margoliouth. Gibb Memorial Series, Vol. VI. 7 vols. Leiden and London, 1907–1927.

———. *Muᶜjam al-buldān*. Ed. F. Wustenfeld. 4 vols. Leipzig, 1866–1873.

Zambaur, Eduard von. *Manuel de généalogie et de chronologie pour l'histoire de l'Islam*. Hanovre, 1927.

INDEX

ᶜAbd Allāh ibn Bībī, 63, 132
ᶜAbd al-Malik ibn Nūḥ, Sāmānid ruler, 124
Abū Bakr Muḥammad ibn ᶜUbayd, 105, 140
Abū al-Faraj, Hamadhānī doctor, 111, 141
Abū al-Fiḍā, 126
Abū Ghālib, the Druggist, 57, 59, 131
Abū al-Ḥasan, the Prosodist, 39, 93, 123
Abū Jaᶜfar, nephew of ᶜAlāᵓ al-Dawla, 130
Abū Kālījār, Būyid ruler, 135, 137
Abū Manṣūr, nephew of ᶜAlāᵓ al-Dawla, 130
Abū Saᶜd ibn Dakhdūl, 53, 128
Abū Saᶜd Muḥammad ibn Ismāᶜīl ibn al-Faḍl, 128
Abū Saᶜīd ibn Abī al-Khayr, 111, 140, 141
Abū Zakariyyā Yaḥyā ibn ᶜAdī, 122
Adharbāyjān, 140
ᶜAḍud al-Dawla, Būyid ruler, 127, 139
Afnan, Soheil M., 11, 13, 117
Afshanah, 17, 119
Aḥmad, S. Maqbūl, 126
al-Ahwānī, A.F., 2, 11, 115, 116
ᶜAlāᵓ al-Dawla, ibn Kākūyah, 57–71 *passim*, 83, 87, 95, 97, 105, 129–36 *passim*, 140
ᶜAlī ibn al-Ḥusayn ibn al-Ḥasanī, 131
ᶜAlī ibn Maᵓmūn, Khwārazm-shāh, 41, 124
ᶜAlid, the, 61, 131
Almagest (of Ptolemy), 25, 45, 121
al-ᶜĀmirī, Abū al-Ḥasan, 113, 141
Anawati, Father G.C., 13, 14, 15, 116, 117
ᶜAnnāz, Abū Shawk Fāris, 11, 53, 128, 133
Arberry, A.J., 11, 12, 13, 116, 117
Aristotle, 33, 55, 93, 105, 109, 121, 122, 141
Arnaldez, R., 120
al-ᶜArūḍī, Abū al-Ḥasan. *See* Abū al-Ḥasan, the Prosodist
Asṭāth, 122
ᶜAufī, Muḥammad, 134
Averroes. *See* Ibn Rushd
al-Azharī, Abū Manṣūr, 71, 134

Baghdād, 51, 109, 124, 127, 134, 137, 139
Bahāᵓ al-Dawla, Būyid ruler, 128
Bahmanyār, 101, 128, 140
Baḥrayn, 134
Balkh, 17, 119, 126
al-Baraqī, Abū Bakr, 11, 39, 93, 123
Barthold, W., 119, 120, 124, 125
Baṣra, 139
Bāṭinīs, 120
Bāwandids, 130
Bāward (Abīward), 41, 125
Bayhaqī, Abū al-Faḍl Muḥammad, 129
Bayhaqī, Ẓahīr al-Dīn. *See* Ibn Funduq
al-Bīrūnī, Abū al-Rayḥān, 103, 119, 124, 140
Blachère, R., 134
Boilot, D.J., 124, 125, 140
Bosworth, C.E., 122–37 *passim.*
Boyle, J.A., 136
Brand, C.M., 117
Brockelmann, C., 115, 116, 123, 134, 139, 141
Browne, E.G., 124, 132
Bukhārā, 17, 19, 21, 35, 41, 119, 123, 124, 141
Būyids, 125, 126, 127, 128, 140
Būzajān, library of, 123

Cahen, C., 119, 134
Canard, M., 120